Prepared In Cooperation with the St. Johns River Water Management District

Geophysical Investigation of Sentinel Lakes in Lake, Seminole, Orange, and Volusia Counties, Florida

By Christopher Reich, James Flocks, and Jeffrey Davis

Open-File Report 2012–1201

U.S. Department of the Interior

U.S. Geological Survey

U.S. Department of the Interior
KEN SALAZAR, Secretary

U.S. Geological Survey
Marcia K. McNutt, Director

U.S. Geological Survey, Reston, Virginia 2012

For more information on the USGS—the Federal source for science about the Earth, its natural and living resources, natural hazards, and the environment, visit *http://www.usgs.gov* or call 1-888-ASK-USGS

For an overview of USGS information products, including maps, imagery, and publications, visit *http://www.usgs.gov/pubprod*

To order this and other USGS information products, visit *http://store.usgs.gov*

Suggested citation:
Reich, Christopher, Flocks, James, and Davis, Jeffrey, 2012, Geophysical investigation of sentinel lakes in Lake, Seminole, Orange, and Volusia Counties, Florida: U.S. Geological Survey Open-File Report 2012-1201, 174 p.

Table of Contents

Figures

Tables

Conversion Factors

Inch/Pound to SI

Multiply	By	To obtain
Length		
foot (ft)	0.3048	meter (m)
mile (mi)	1.609	kilometer (km)
yard (yd)	0.9144	meter (m)
Area		
acre	4,047	square meter (m2)
square foot (ft2)	0.09290	square meter (m2)
square inch (in2)	6.452	square centimeter (cm2)
Volume		
gallon (gal)	3.785	liter (L)
gallon (gal)	0.003785	cubic meter (m3)
cubic inch (in3)	0.01639	liter (L)
Hydraulic conductivity		
foot per day (ft/d)	0.3048	meter per day (m/d)

Temperature in degrees Celsius (°C) may be converted to degrees Fahrenheit (°F) as follows:

°F=(1.8×°C)+32

Temperature in degrees Fahrenheit (°F) may be converted to degrees Celsius (°C) as follows:

°C=(°F-32)/1.8

Vertical coordinate information is referenced to the North American Vertical Datum of 1988 (NAVD88)

Geophysical Investigation of Sentinel Lakes in Lake, Seminole, Orange, and Volusia Counties, Florida

By Christopher Reich, James Flocks, and Jeffrey Davis

Abstract

This study was initiated in cooperation with the St. Johns River Water Management District (SJRWMD) to investigate groundwater and surface-water interaction in designated sentinel lakes in central Florida. Sentinel lakes are a SJRWMD established set of priority water bodies (lakes) for which minimum flows and levels (MFLs) are determined. Understanding both the structure and lithology beneath these lakes can ultimately lead to a better understanding of the MFLs and why water levels fluctuate in certain lakes more so than in other lakes. These sentinel lakes have become important water bodies to use as water-fluctuation indicators in the SJRWMD Minimum Flows and Levels program and will be used to define long-term hydrologic and ecologic performance measures. Geologic control on lake hydrology remains poorly understood in this study area. Therefore, the U.S. Geological Survey investigated 16 of the 21 water bodies on the SJRWMD priority list. Geologic information was obtained by the tandem use of high-resolution seismic profiling (HRSP) and direct-current (DC) resistivity profiling to isolate both the geologic framework (structure) and composition (lithology). Previous HRSP surveys from various lakes in the study area have been successful in identifying karst features, such as subsidence sinkholes. However, by using this method only, it is difficult to image highly irregular or chaotic surfaces, such as collapse sinkholes. Resistivity profiling was used to complement HRSP by detecting porosity change within fractured or collapsed structures and increase the ability to fully characterize the subsurface.

Lake Saunders (Lake County) is an example of a lake composed of a series of north-south-trending sinkholes that have joined to form one lake body. HRSP shows surface depressions and deformation in the substrate. Resistivity data likewise show areas in the southern part of the lake where resistivity shifts abruptly from approximately 400 ohm meters (ohm-m) along the edges to approximately 12 ohm-m in the center. These well-defined areas may indicate a 'ravel' zone of increased porosity or clay content. Within Lake Helen (Volusia County), a parallel set of seismic reflectors within a host of chaotic reflectors may represent fill within a large sinkhole. The feature extends to more than 50 meters (m) deep and contains very steep pinnacles within the center. Seismic data in Lake Helen are supported by high resistivity values from adjacent continuous resistivity profiles that show possible center collapse within the lake and infilling of sandy material. When used together, HRSP and DC resistivity techniques provide a composite image of structure and lithology to detect potential conduits for fluid flow.

Introduction

The central Florida lake region is unique because there are an estimated 7,800 lakes differing from one another in their geologic development. The lakes in central Florida are created by the dissolution (chemical weathering) of buried limestone, a process known as karstification. As karst forms, the sand and clay overburden begins to ravel (physically weather) into open pores and caverns in the limestone, leaving a depression at the land surface (Beck, 1988; Schiffer, 1998; Kindinger and others, 1999). The degree of karst development, as well as other factors including significant overburden, can lead to the formation of either subsidence- or collapse-type sinkholes, which are the primary types of sinkholes found in this study area (Schiffer, 1998; Kindinger and others, 1999). Over time, the sinkholes collect enough fine material in the 'throat' of the feature to allow for the containment of water, which eventually will form lakes. Some lakes are conglomerates of small sinkholes that co-join and lead to the formation of large, irregular-shaped lakes such as Lake Jessup in Seminole County (fig. 1; Kindinger and others, 2000).

In 2007, the SJRWMD developed a priority list of sentinel lakes that are incorporated within the Minimum Flows and Levels (MFL) program. These sentinel lakes have become important water bodies in the program and will be used to define long-term hydrologic and ecologic performance measures (SJRWMD, 2008). This study was initiated in cooperation with the St. Johns River Water Management District (SJRWMD) to investigate 16 of the 21 water bodies on the SJRWMD priority list (fig. 1; Johns Lake comprises 4 water bodies)

2

The primary objective of this study was to conduct geophysical surveys in designated sentinel lakes and provide geologic information. High-resolution seismic profiling (HRSP) and direct-

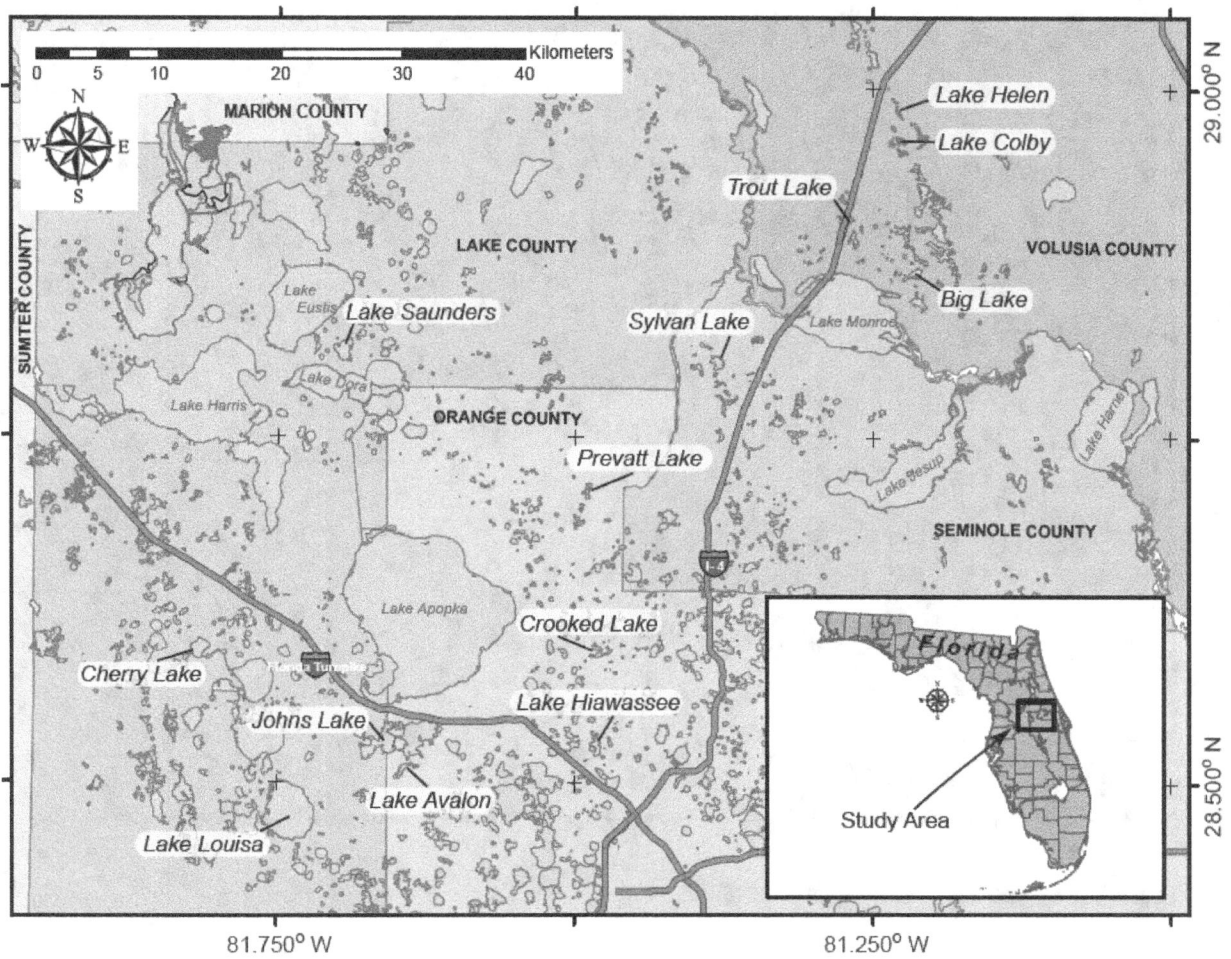

Figure 1. Map shows location of sentinel lakes surveyed in this central Florida study.

current (DC) resistivity methods were used in tandem to isolate both geologic framework (structure) and composition (lithology). All of the lakes surveyed in this study are located in the Central Lakes District (fig. 2), a physiographic region of Florida designated by the surficial geology and occurrence of numerous lakes.

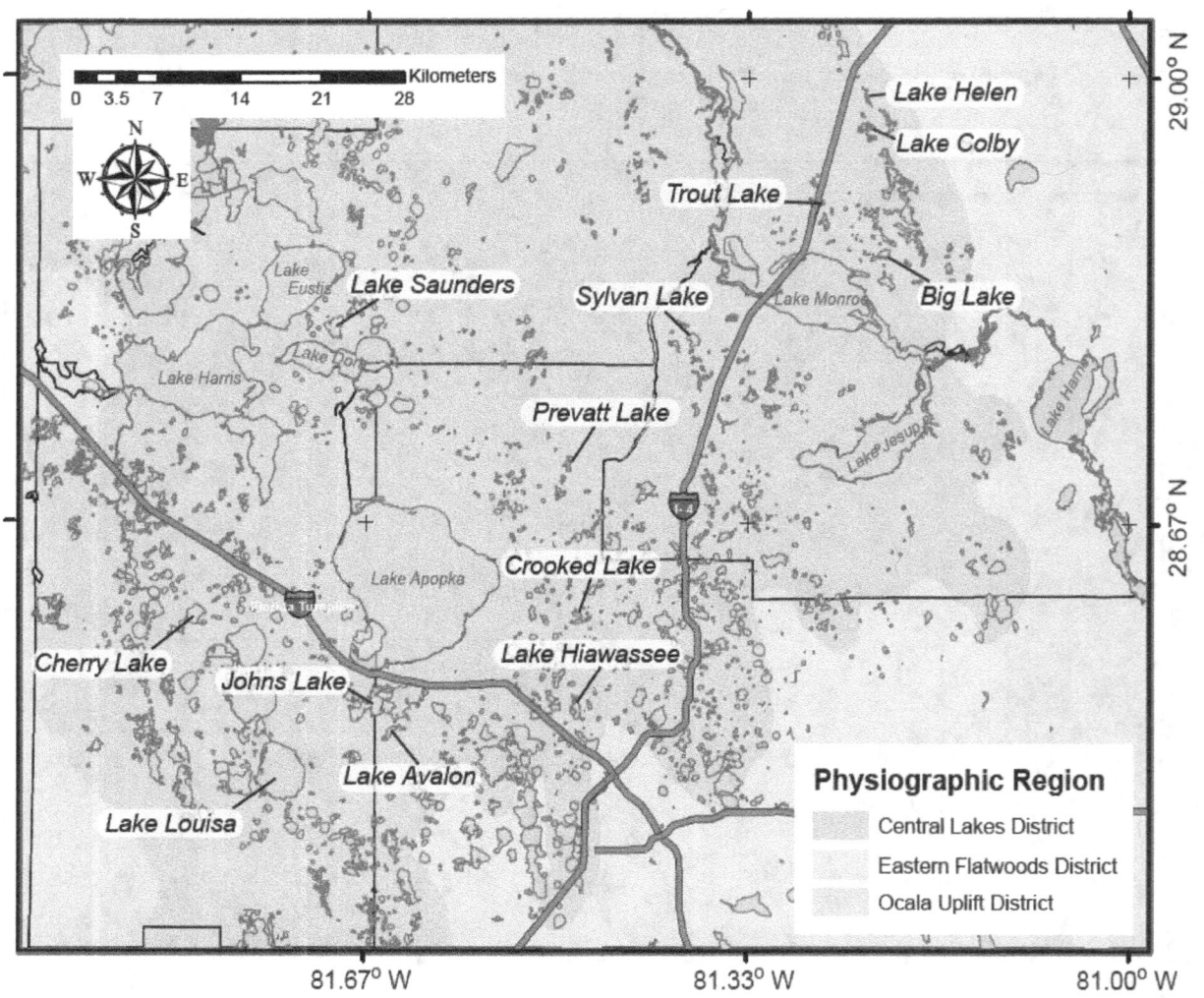

Figure 2. Physiographic regions of central Florida.

Methods

High-Resolution Seismic Profiling

Seismic-reflection profiling is a technique used to acoustically map the structural features of the seafloor and subsurface. Seismic data are collected continuously to provide a two-dimensional profile of the subsurface. This technique is useful to map the thickness and spatial extent of lithologic units, map structural features such as subsidence or collapse sinkholes, and measure depths to subsurface horizons. High-resolution seismic profiling (HRSP) equipment consists of an electro-magnetic ("boomer") plate, towed behind a vessel at a rate of about 4 knots (fig. 3A). The plate is attached to a catamaran sled that floats on the water surface. The plate is electronically triggered every 500 milliseconds (ms) to create a broadband acoustic frequency between 2 and 6 kilohertz (kHz) and a power source between 100 and 300 Joules (J). The signal propagates into the subbottom and is reflected proportional to the different densities within the stratigraphy. The acoustic return is detected by a multi-element hydrophone array on the water surface and transmitted to a topside computer for signal processing. Each transmitted signal (trace) is stacked horizontally to produce a seismic profile (fig. 3B).

This seismic data-collection technique was originally developed for marine applications. Since the 1990s, the system has been adapted through an iterative process to function in the small lakes and narrow canals of central and south Florida. Adjustments in field techniques and process-

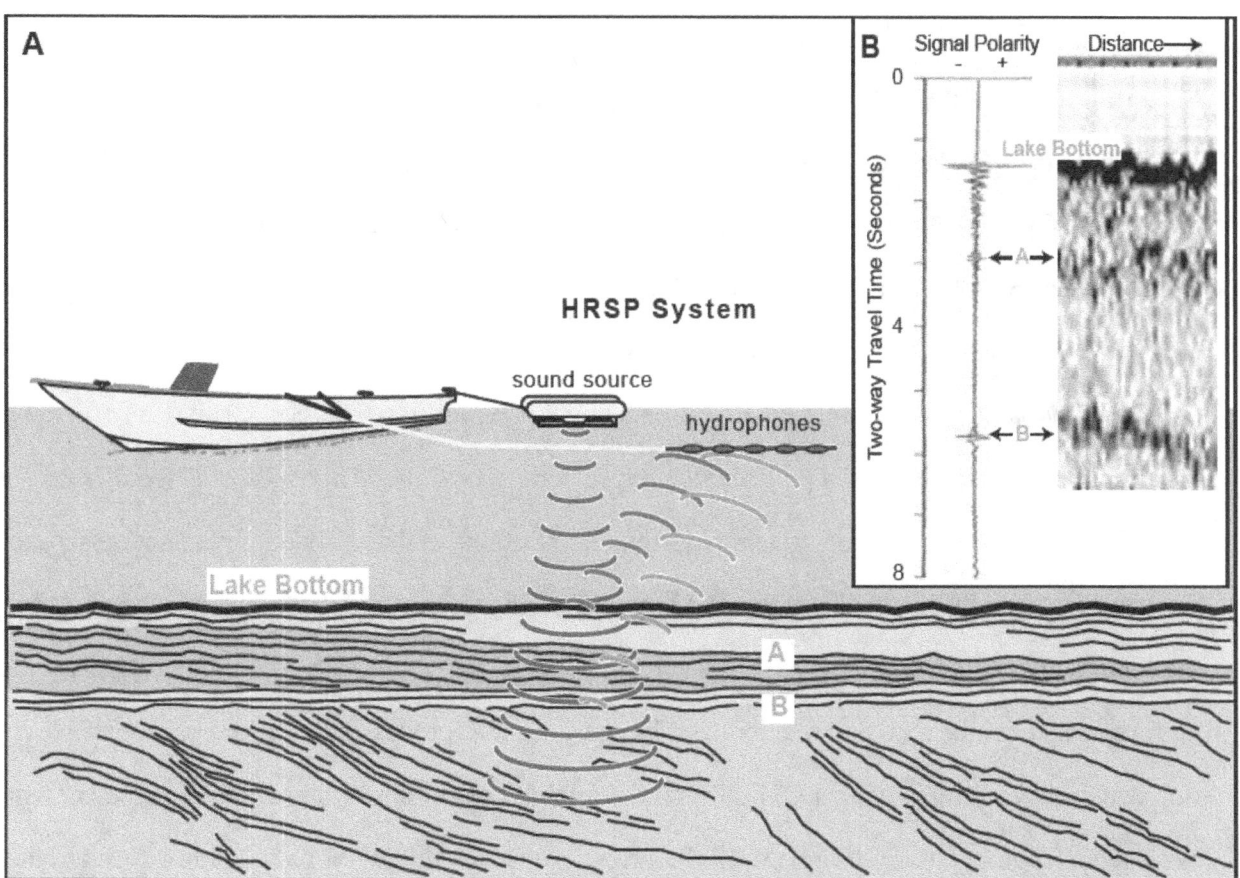

Figure 3. Schematic of seismic data collection (A) and example profile (B). HRSP, high-resolution seismic profiling.

ing are necessary to obtain suitable data, depending on location. Variations in data acquisition and processing techniques are described in various publications (table 1).

Table 1. Selected publications using high-resolution seismic profiling in Florida. Full citations can be found in the references section.

Author	Location
Flocks and others (2001)	Indian River Lagoon, Fla.
Harrison and others (2007)	Offshore Siesta Key, Fla.
Kindinger (2002)	Miami-Dade County, Fla.
Kindinger and others (1994)	Orange Lake, Alachua County, Fla.
Kindinger and others (1999)	Various lakes, north-central Florida
Reich and others (2001)	Crescent Beach Spring, St. Johns County, Fla.

Seismic profiles were collected using a single-channel Triton Elics Delph High-Resolution Seismic-Profile System. Proprietary hardware and software for the Triton Elics system were run in real time on a PC laptop (Windows XP). Digital data were stored on an internal hard disk and backed up on a CD-ROM. The acoustic source was an electromechanical device, a Geopulse Model 5420A Power Supply firing an Applied Acoustics AA300 Boomer Plate mounted on a catamaran sled. Power settings were 100 to 280 J depending upon data quality during acquisition. The "Boomer" is a broadband acoustic source with a frequency range of 2.0 to 6.0 kHz. A NextGen 10-channel hydrophone streamer was used to detect the return acoustical pulse. This pulse was fed directly into the Triton Elics Delph Seismic system for storage. Variations in data collection were necessary to improve data quality as physiography and lithology changed. Seismic data were saved and stored in the Society of Exploration Geophysicists (SEG Y) format (Barry and others, 1975), a standard digital format that can be read and manipulated by most seismic-processing software packages. Navigation data were collected using a CSI Differential Global Positioning System (DGPS) receiver using Wide Area Augmentation System (WAAS) correction. Differential GPS navigation was fed to the seismic-acquisition system every second by a WAAS/Beacon DGPS receiver. The accuracy of this receiver is to within 5 meters (m). These edited results were used to generate trackline maps. The shotpoint data have not been corrected to reflect the offset between the source and the GPS antenna. Position fixes for every 500 shots and for the start of line are also provided as an aide for easy registering of the data after projection (Harrison and others, 2009a).

Field Activities

Each field excursion is given a unique field activity number that includes a two-digit year identifier, a three-digit activity, project, or program identifier and a two-digit 'cruise leg' number (for example, 08LCA01 stands for the first leg of the Leaky Coastal Aquifer project in 2008). Under each activity are individual geophysical line numbers including a two-digit year identifier, acquisition tool (b for Boomer), and two digit line number (for example, 08b01). In this project a seismic survey was followed by a DC-resistivity survey, and then a subsequent seismic survey; thus, there are three legs to this project (for example, 08LCA01, 02, and 03).

Boomer Data Processing

The raw SEG Y data were processed using Seismic Unix (SU) to produce the Graphics Interchange Format (GIF) seismic profiles included in this report. A representative data processing sequence consisted of (1) bandpass filter: 300-500-2,500-3,000 hertz (Hz), (2) automatic gain control, (3) PostScript display at 15 milliseconds per inch (ms/in.) and 215 shots/in., and (4) converted PostScript files to GIF format (Harrison and others, 2009a).

Data Interpretation

The Triton Elics Delph Geophysical system measures and displays two-way travel time (TWT) of the acoustical pulse in ms. Amplitude and velocity of the signal are affected by variations in lithology of the underlying strata. Laterally consistent amplitude changes (lithologic contacts or correlations of acoustic impedance in similar lithologies) are displayed as continuous reflections on the seismic profiles. Depth to reflection is determined from the TWT and adjusted to the subsurface velocity of the signal. Carbonates have a wide range of velocities such as those reported by refraction studies conducted in areas within Alachua County, Fla., ranging from 1,707 to 4,939 meters per second (m/s) (5,599 to 16,200 feet per second, ft/s) for the Hawthorn Group (Wiener, 1982). Wiener (1982) reported lower velocities for sand and clay sediments. Suggested compressional velocities for Hawthorn Group sediments for the Florida Platform range from 1,500 to 1,800 m/s (4,920 to 5,904 ft/s; Sacks and others, 1991; Kindinger and others, 1999, 2000). Measured depths to known stratigraphic horizons provide sound velocities through the Hawthorn Group. Figure 4 shows a correlation of depth-to-horizon compared between gamma log profile measurements obtained from nearby monitor wells and seismic profiles for the top of the Ocala Limestone in the study area (Kindinger and others, 1999). A best-fit curve through the data provides a velocity of 1,950 m/s. Due to the vertical variability of the geology in this area (for example, Hawthorn Group clays and silts versus Ocala Limestone), a mid-range velocity TWT of 2,000 m/s (6,560 ft/s) is used.

More than 100 line-kilometers (line-km) of seismic data were collected from 10 lakes (fig. 1 and table 2). Quality of profile data varied between good to poor depending on numerous variations in structure and lithology. Typically, where water depths were exceedingly shallow (<1.25 m) or abundant submerged aquatic vegetation was present, the signal quality was significantly deteriorated.

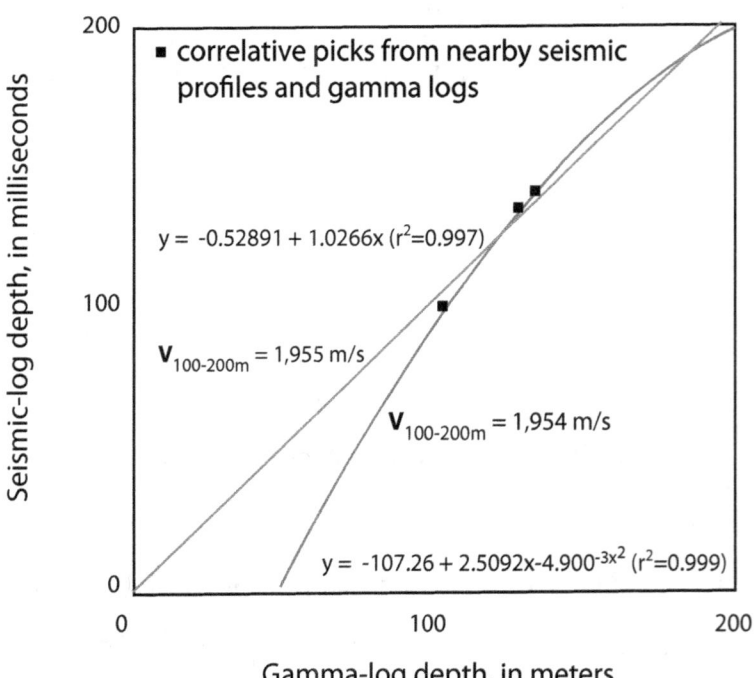

Figure 4. Plot of depth-to-horizon in milliseconds on seismic profiles versus depth-to-peak in meters on natural gamma logs from sites acquired in northeast Florida. The resulting equations from the best-fit curve (blue) or the best-fit curve with zero origin (red) were used to calculate sound velocity. m/s, meters per second.

8

Direct-Current Resistivity

DC resistivity was used in the study of 11 sentinel lakes of Lake, Seminole, Orange, and Volusia Counties (fig. 1 and table 2). Two different modes of resistivity were used in this investigation: boat-towed continuous resistivity profiling system (CRP) and land-based stationary system. Each system utilizes the same Supersting R8/IP control box (Advanced Geosciences, Inc., AGI); however, the firmware must be changed to operate the two different cables.

Resistivity varies widely in natural systems and is influenced by a multitude of physical parameters such as temperature, specific conductivity (salinity) of pore fluids, lithology, and porosity. The DC resistivity system measures bulk resistivity that can lead to ambiguities in interpreting the data. Only through field investigations (ground-truthing) can a correct interpretation be resolved. Prior knowledge of the geology and hydrology of an area and calibration by towing the CRP streamer over established underwater monitoring wells or locating a stationary resistivity line near existing wells are beneficial in interpreting resistivity profiles.

CRP was conducted on the lakes that were large enough and had deep enough water to operate a boat and tow the 100-m-long cable. The lakes chosen for CRP were Avalon, Cherry, Helen, Hiawassee, Johns, Louisa, Saunders, and Sylvan. The boat-towed cable has 11 electrodes with a 10-m electrode spacing that allows for the collection of an electrical-resistivity image to a depth of approximately 25 m. The Supersting R8/IP injects a current of up to 2 amps and power of 200 watts. In CRP mode, the Supersting unit can simultaneously measure eight channels while injecting a current at a rate of 1 to 3 s. The first two electrodes produce the current, and the remaining nine measure the resulting voltage potential. The boat tows the cable, suspended by swimming pool floats, along the surface of the water, and an apparent resistivity profile (tomograph) with eight simultaneous measurement points, each at a different apparent depth (0 to 25 m), is constructed (fig. 5).

Land-based stationary resistivity was used to investigate smaller areas and with much greater resolution than CRP. Prevatt, Crooked, and Colby Lakes were investigated using the land-based stationary cable. The stationary cable is 112 m long and contains 56 electrodes at a 2-m

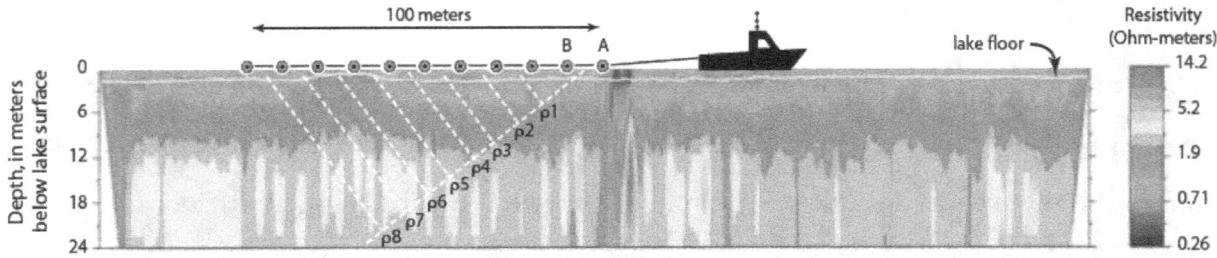

Figure 5. Boat-towed continuous resistivity profile system shows location of current electrodes (A and B) and remaining potential electrodes (unlabeled) and approximate position of measured resistivity (ρ1-ρ8).

spacing. The stationary cable is controlled through an external switch box that permits eight channels (electrodes) to operate simultaneously (fig. 6). The pre-programmed command file instructs the switch box as to the order in which the electrodes are activated. A run with a forward-reverse array, used to lower the reciprocal errors and enhance the resolution, takes approximately 1 hour. After the collection of data, elevations at each of the electrodes are collected using a laser-level and bar-coded staffing rod. The elevations can be entered into a terrain file, which the EarthImager 2D software can read and thereby correct the electrode position during the data-inversion process. If the cable is split between land and water, which occurs often, the position of the water can be included in the terrain file.

Processing CRP and land-based stationary data was accomplished by using AGI Earth Imager 2D software. EarthImager 2D uses a finite-element forward-modeling method with the smooth-model L2-normalized inversion and an average apparent-resistivity starting model. The program does not use reciprocal errors in CRP mode due to the fact that the electrodes cannot be stacked or reversed rapidly enough before they have moved while being towed. In land-based mode, however, reciprocal measurements are collected in order to lower the measured errors. Minimum and maximum resistivity values were set at 1 and 1,000 ohm meters (ohm-m), respectively. Although surface-water conductivity and temperature data were collected, the surface-water column in the CRP profiles was not fixed in the processing of the resistivity data. Day-Lewis and others (2006)

Figure 6. Photograph shows the Supersting system that was used in the collection of land-based stationary resistivity. A, Supersting R8/IP box; B, switch box; C, connector end of the 56 electrode cable; D, battery.

have shown that entering an incorrect surface-water resistivity can lead to large errors in interpreted resistivity profiles. The goodness of fit of the model was determined by the lowest model root mean square error (RMS). The lowest RMS was achieved by allowing the water column to be processed during the inversion process. However, surface-water conductivity was measured during stationary-resistivity data collection and therefore the surface water was fixed during the inversion process. This works well in smaller areas where surface-water temperature and conductivity do not fluctuate drastically enough to influence the resistivity-inversion process.

Results and Discussion

The lakes investigated in this study (fig. 1 and table 2) will be discussed individually and include information from both HRSP and DC resistivity.

Table 2. List of sentinel lakes surveyed in this study of central Florida.

[HRSP, high-resolution seismic profiling; CRP, continuous resistivity profiling; LBR, land-based resistivity. Data acquired in 2008, month/day for HRSP shown. HRSP data published as data archives: Harrison and others, 2009a, and Harrison and others, 2009b]

Lake Name	County	Survey Method[†]	Latitude (N)	Longitude (W)
Lake Avalon	Orange	HRSP (3/28); CRP	81.6417	28.5125
Big Lake	Volusia	HRSP (3/26)	81.2128	28.8689
Cherry Lake	Lake	HRSP (9/4); CRP	81.8167	28.5919
Lake Colby	Volusia	HRSP (3/24); LBR	81.2325	28.9642
Crooked Lake	Orange	LBR	81.4786	28.5958
Lake Helen	Volusia	HRSP (3/24); CRP	81.2300	28.9842
Lake Hiawassee	Orange	CRP	81.4825	28.5280
Johns Lake	Orange	HRSP (3/27); CRP	81.6330	28.5350
Lake Louisa	Lake	CRP	81.7383	28.4797
Prevatt Lake	Orange	LBR	81.4900	28.7119
Lake Saunders	Lake	HRSP (3/25); CRP	81.6958	28.8122
Sylvan Lake	Seminole	CRP	81.3805	28.8047
Trout Lake	Volusia	HRSP (3/25)	81.2686	28.9072

Lake Avalon

Seismic Profiles

Lake Avalon is located in Orange County and is primarily surrounded by an agricultural community with a few residential homes along the lake edge. Lake Avalon, located in the Central Lakes District, has an elongate shape and is clustered with several similar lakes (including Johns Lake). Studies in this area have shown this lake configuration typically represents small individual sinkholes, joined by dissolution valleys (Kindinger and others, 2000). Twenty HRSP lines were acquired across the central portion of the lake (fig. 7). Seismic profiles (08b126 and 08b135) from the lake are shown in figure 8. The lake bottom can be determined from the seismic data, and a bathymetric map generated from the seismic data is shown in figure 9. The subsurface data are characterized by significant noise, obscuring features at depth. However, the seismic profiles show a consistent high-amplitude reflector below the lake bottom (fig. 8) that persists laterally on several profiles (fig. 10). This mappable horizon is interpreted to be a karst surface or significant deformation of overburden on top of an underlying karst surface. A map of this feature (fig. 11) shows several depressions in the subsurface that could represent conduits linking surface water and groundwater.

Continuous Resistivity Profiles

CRP was conducted on Lake Avalon from near the northeast corner, south and southwest toward a shallow reed line approximately one-half the distance across the lake. Approximately 2.6 kilometers (km) of resistivity data were collected, which are shown in five separate profiles (appendix, pages A1-A6; fig. 12). There are several distinct features in the profiles that indicate either collapse

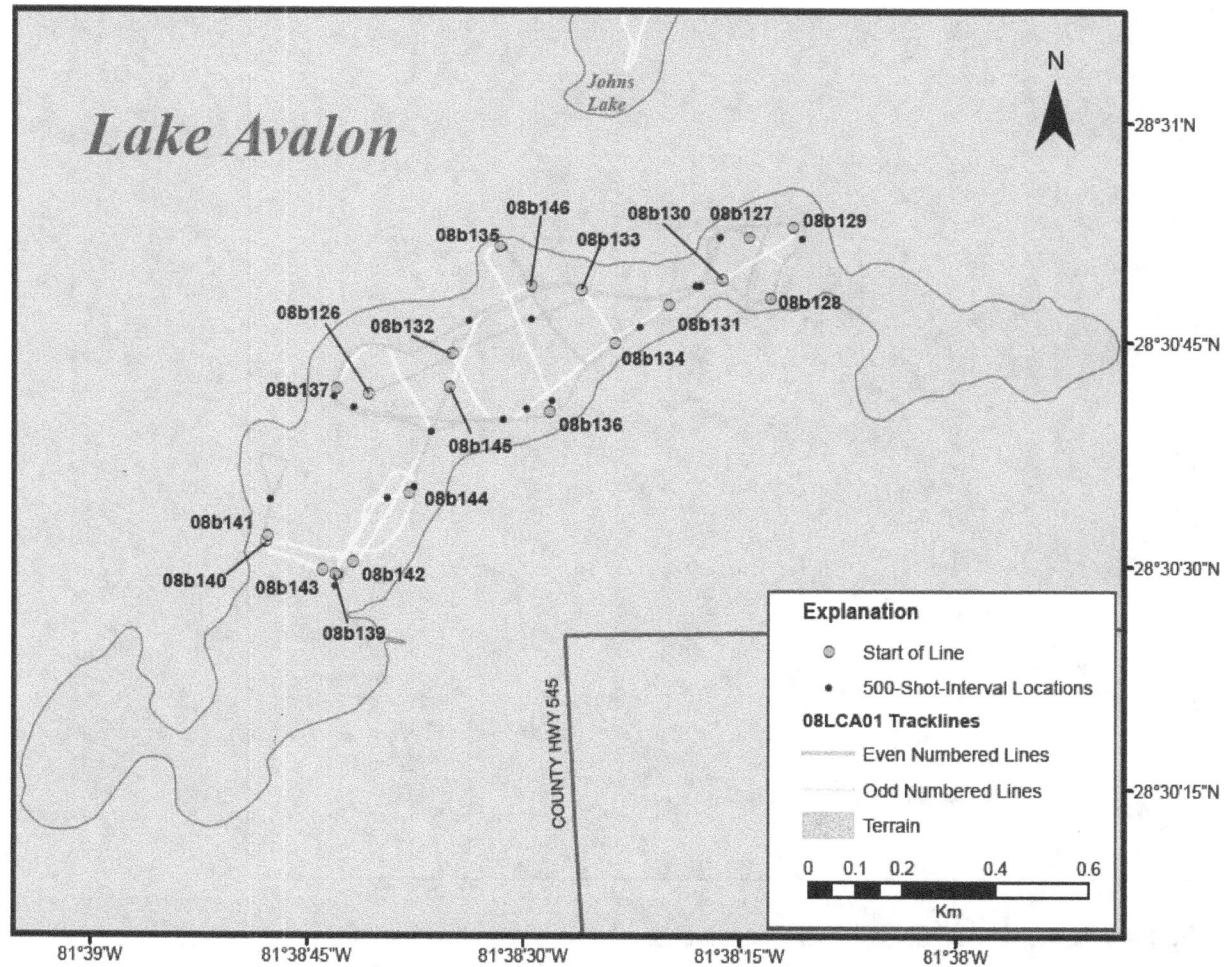

Figure 7. Seismic-profile tracklines collected in Lake Avalon.

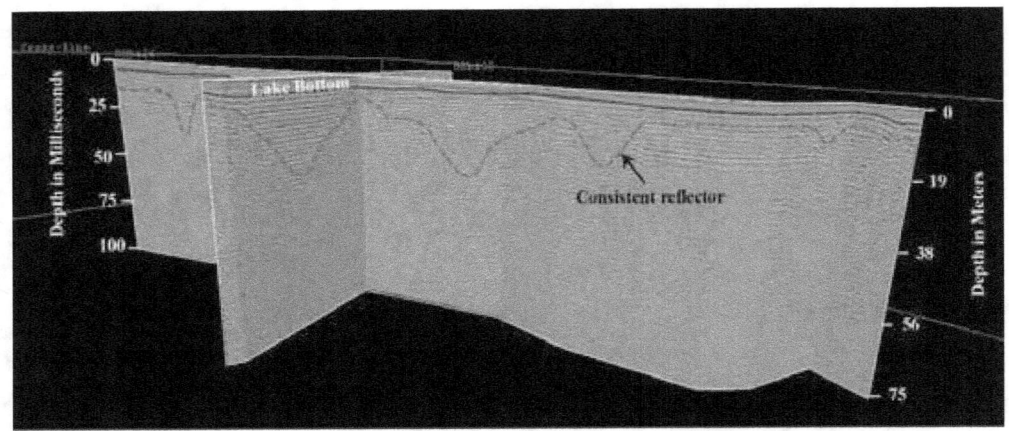

Figure 8. Example seismic profile collected in Lake Avalon. Locations of lines 08B126 and 08b135 are shown in figure 7.

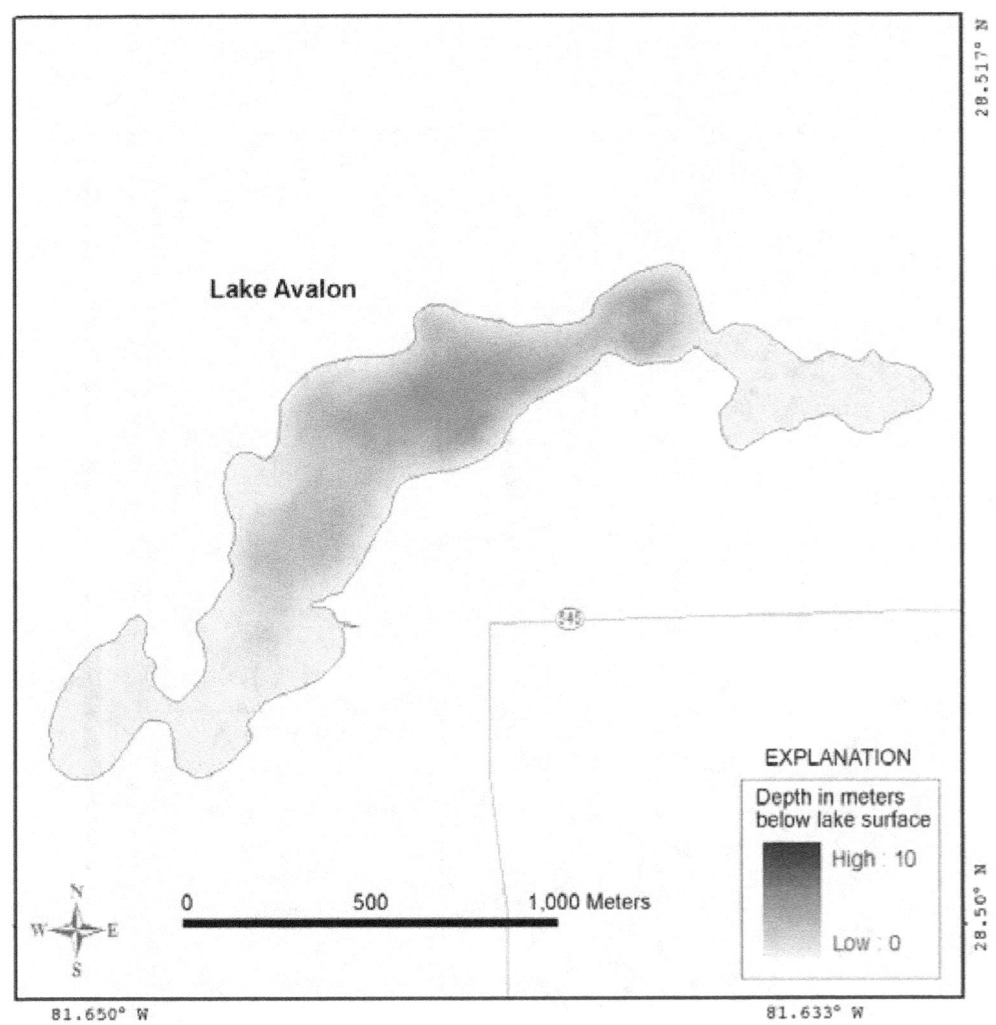

Figure 9. Bathymetric map of the lake bottom, Lake Avalon, interpreted from seismic profiles. Refer to figure 7 for trackline coverage because not all of the lake was surveyed.

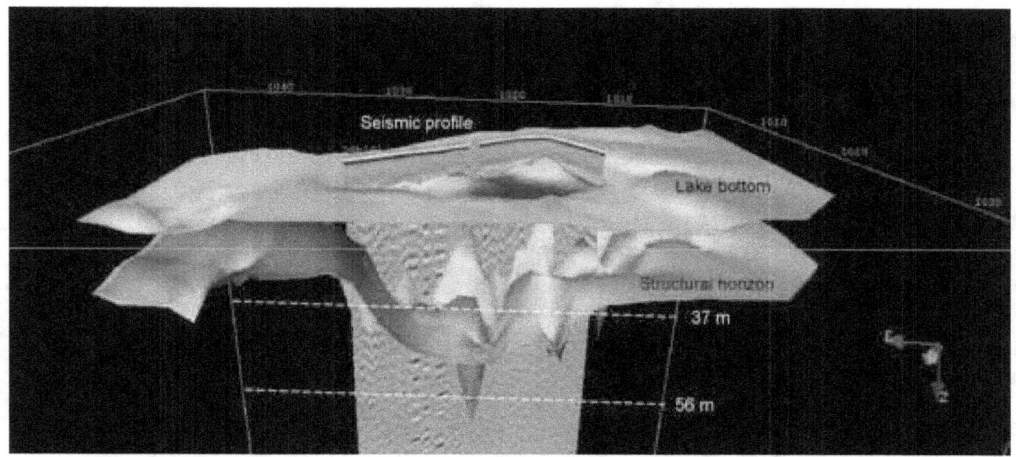

Figure 10. Three-dimensional perspective of a structural horizon below Lake Avalon, interpreted from seismic profiles, characteristic of a karst surface.

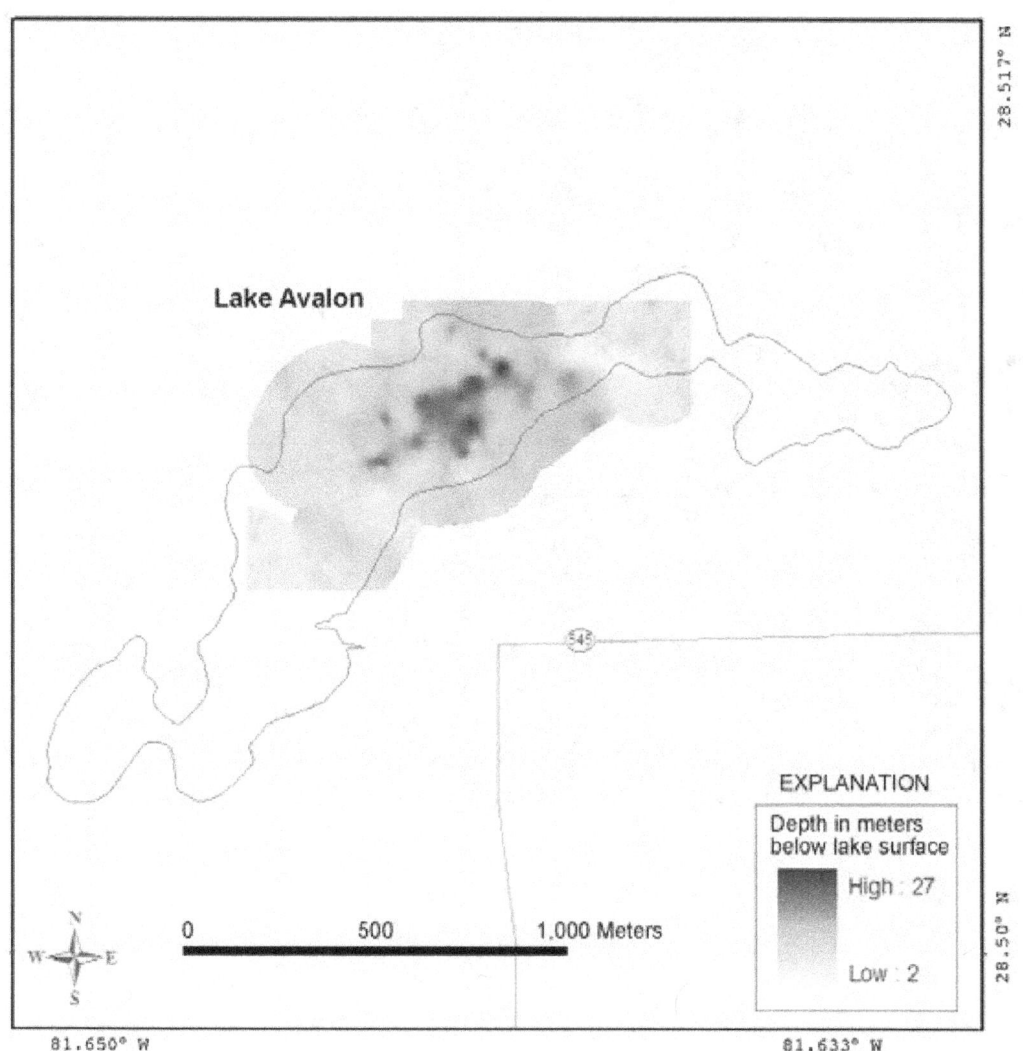

Figure 11. Color-shaded relief map of a structural horizon below Lake Avalon, interpreted from seismic profiles (see red line in figure 8).

or subsidence features. The change in resistivity in these features may correlate to structural features that are presently infilled (fig. 13). These areas are typically known as ravel zones and represent areas where subsidence or collapse in the deep subsurface has allowed for the downward movement of overlying sediments. Ravel zones are typically represented by a decrease in resistivity (~50-100 ohm-m) because of increased porosity (Dobecki and Upchurch, 2006); however, in many of the lakes discussed in this report, resistivity is high in the throats, indicating infilling of quartz sands.

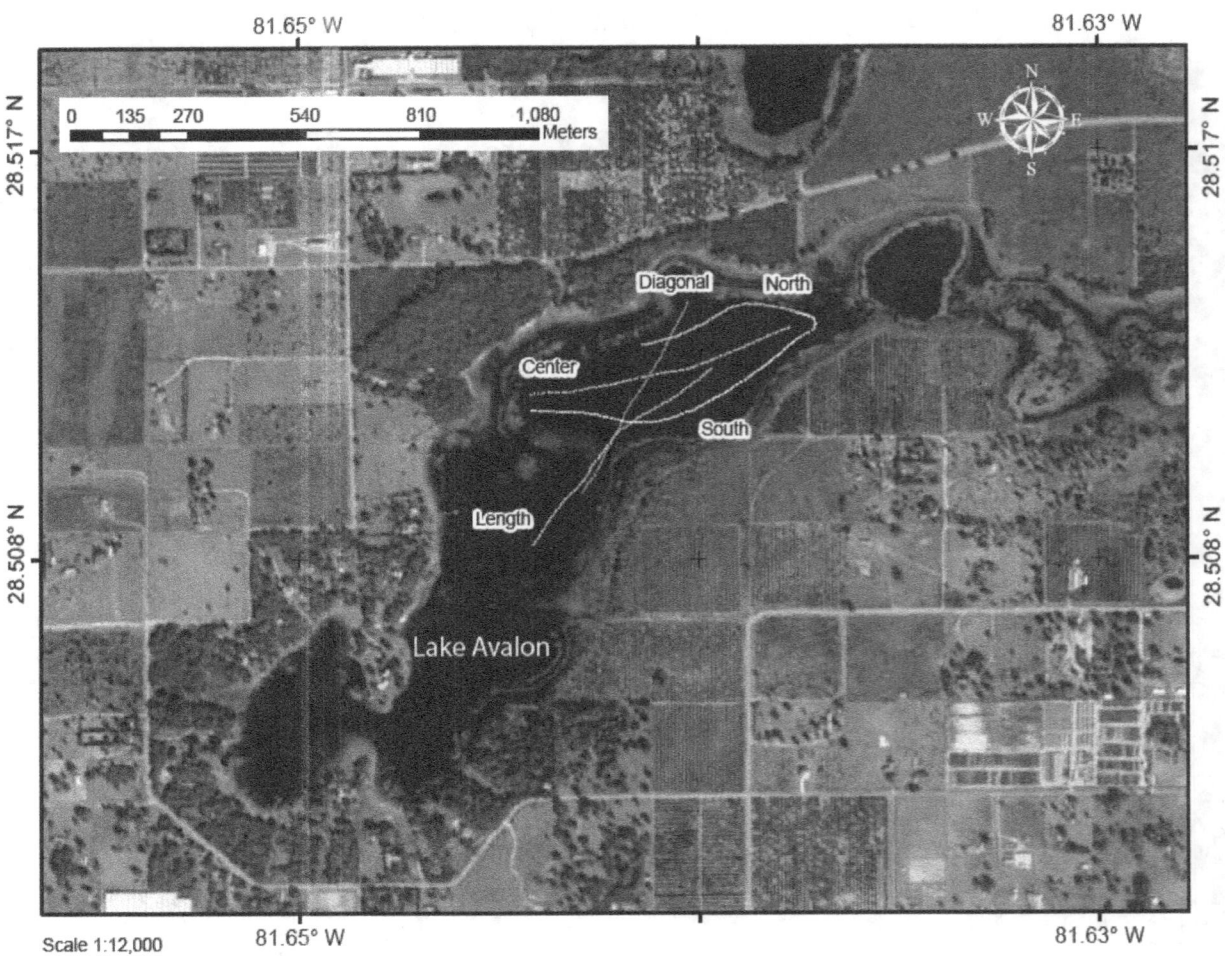

Figure 12. Map shows continuous resistivity profile tracklines for Lake Avalon.

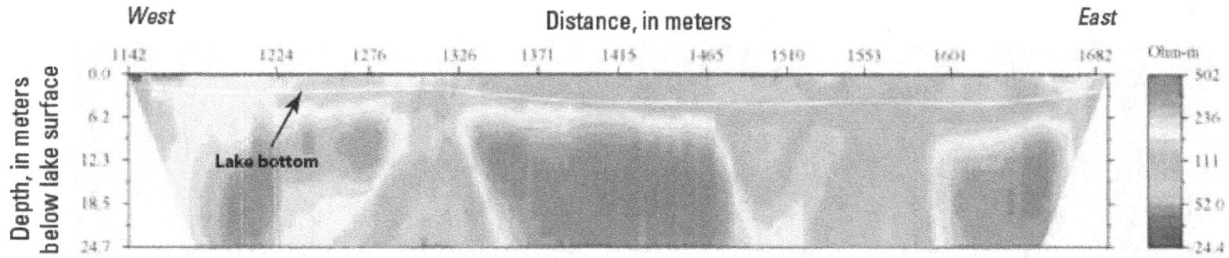

Figure 13. Resistivity profile (Avalon_Center) from Lake Avalon presents an example of potential collapse features (high-resistivity areas in red) and subsequent infilling of overburden (low resistivity represented by green and blue). Ohm-m, ohm meters.

Big Lake

Seismic Profiles

Big Lake is an oval-shaped lake situated among a cluster of similarly shaped lakes. Numerous lakes within this Central Lakes District occupy the lower elevations of sand hills with summits generally between 24 and 30 m (Kindinger and others, 2000) and represent sinks that penetrate the underlying Ocala Limestone and Floridan Aquifer system. Seismic profiles from Big Lake (fig. 14) are predominantly obscured at depth (fig. 15). Figure 15 shows high-angle reflectors at the peripheries of lake-bottom depressions. The contrast of layered acoustic signal in the depressions, versus the adjacent more chaotic signal, may be related to collapse and fill of the Hawthorn Group into deeper Ocala Limestone strata. Due to the chaotic nature of the signal, subsurface features could not be mapped. The bathymetry of the lake (fig. 16) shows the depressions in the lake bottom, which can be correlated to the structural features observed in figure 15.

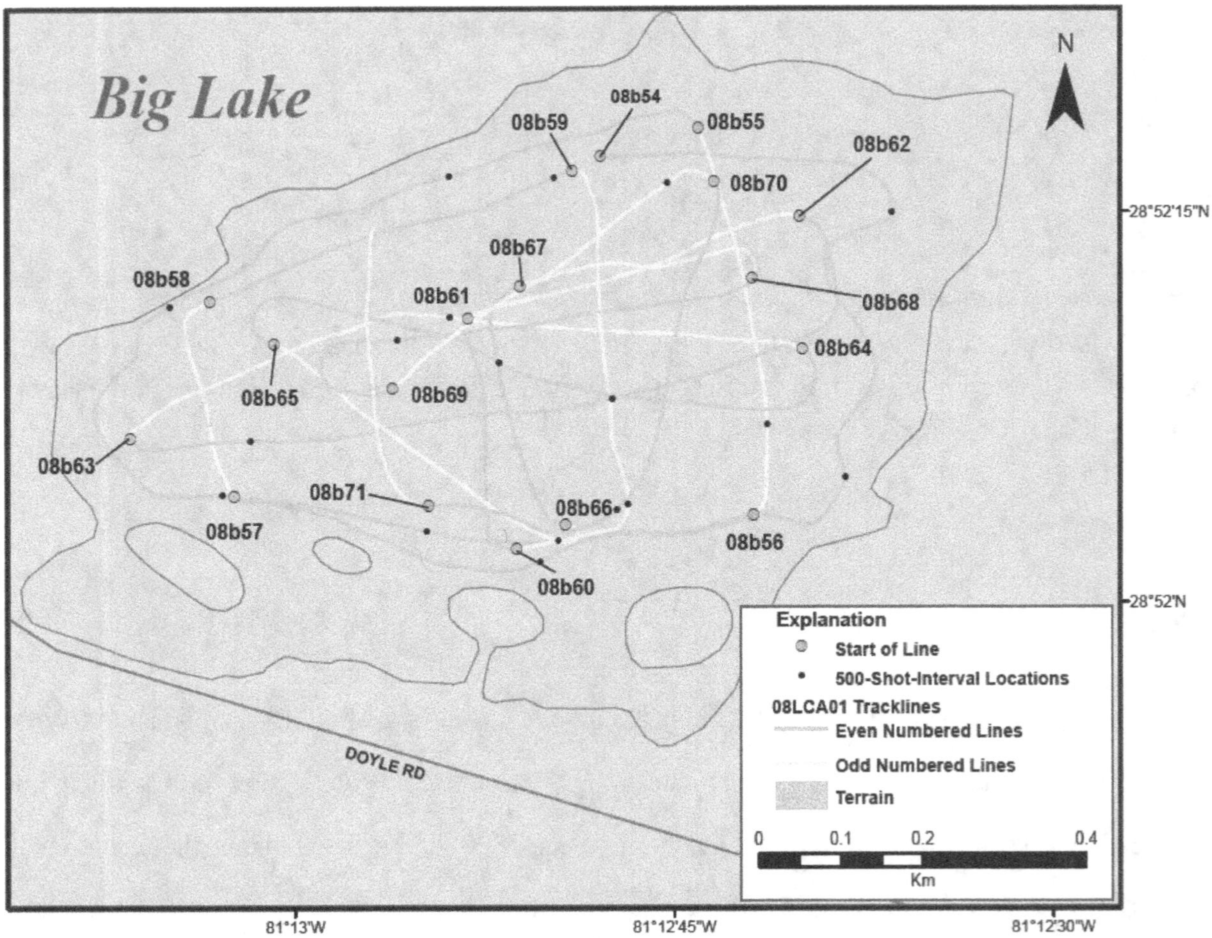

Figure 14. Map shows seismic-profile tracklines for Big Lake.

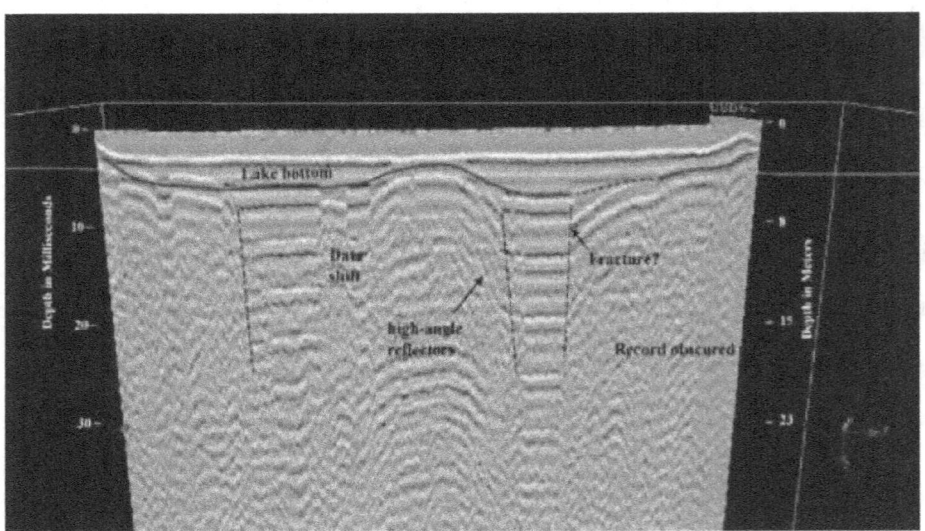

Figure 15. Seismic profile (08b62) collected in Big Lake. Location of line 08b62 is shown in figure 14.

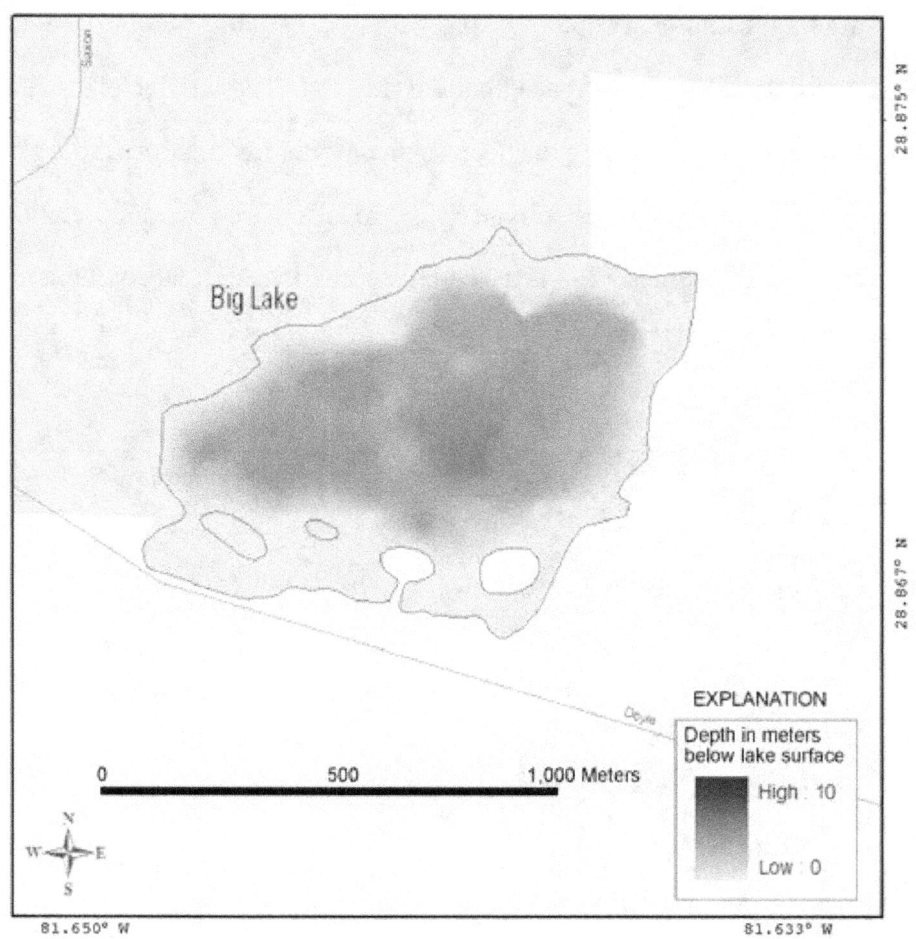

Figure 16. Bathymetric map of the lake bottom, Big Lake, interpreted from seismic profiles.

Cherry Lake

Seismic Profiles

Cherry Lake, located in Lake County, is nearly circular with a small inlet on the southeastern shore and a control structure and levee on the western shore. Cherry Lake occurs in a depression and is bordered by flanking highlands. The lake is accompanied by several adjoining sinkholes. Figure 17 shows the locations of seismic profiles collected from the lake. Seismic-data quality is poor due to electrical noise in the data, which occurred during acquisition. However, the lake bottom can still be determined from the seismic profiles (fig. 18), which show a depression in the center of the lake. Disruptions in the reflectors at the flank of this depression are consistent across profiles (fig.

19) and may be related to structural collapse at depth. The profiles show a highly variable bottom and a consistent pattern of horizontal reflectors in the subbottom (fig. 19). These reflectors may be associated with unconsolidated material infilling the depression or with deformation of the clay units in the Hawthorn Group. Figure 20 shows the bathymetry of the lake, based on interpretation of the lake bottom obtained from seismic profiles. The lake-bottom depressions correlate with deformation in the subsurface.

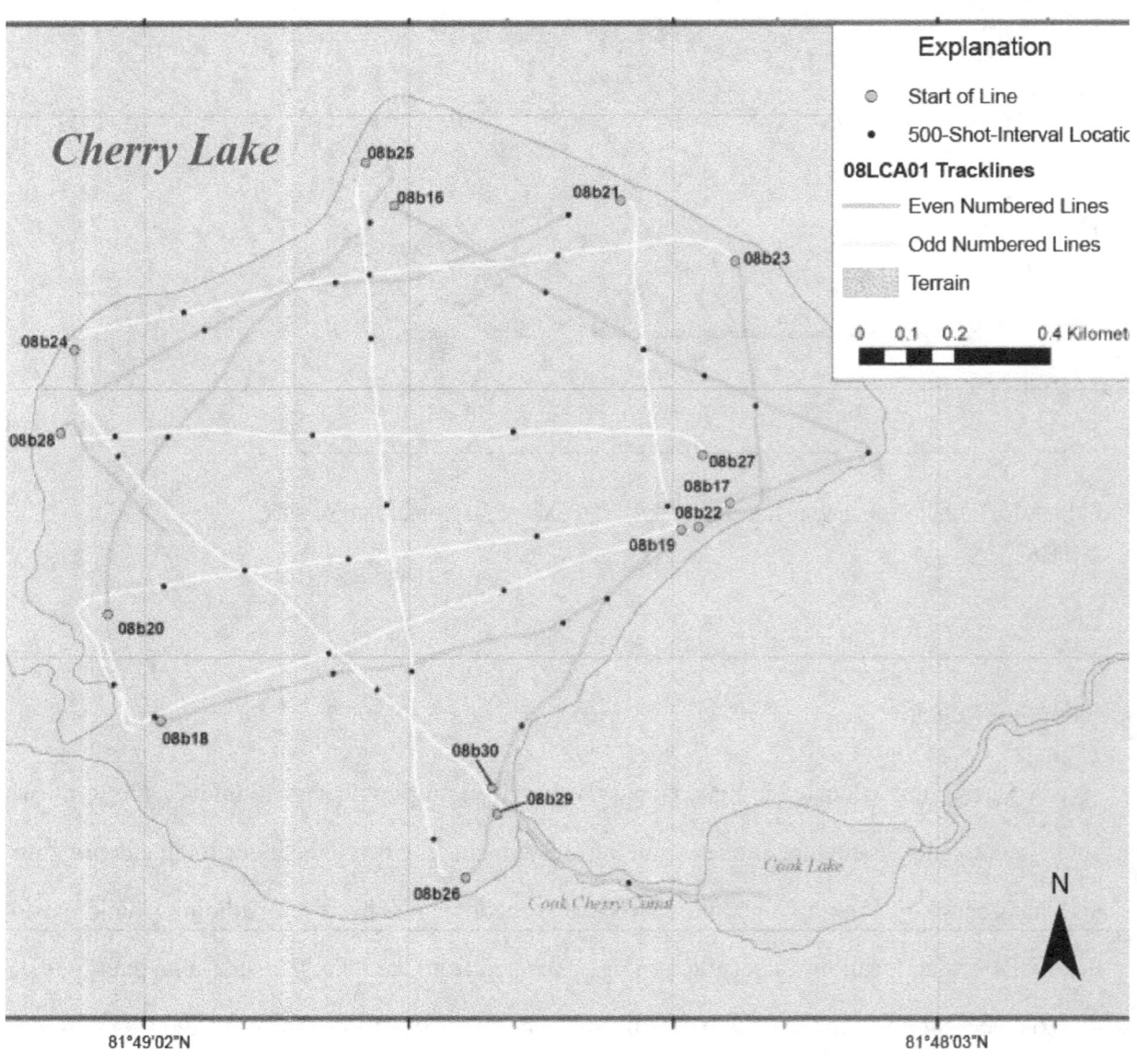

Figure 17. Map shows seismic-profile tracklines for Cherry Lake.

Figure 18. Seismic profile (08b17) collected in Cherry Lake. Location of line 08b17 is shown in figure 17. Because of the acoustic noise in the profile, the figure has been color enhanced to refine the near-surface data.

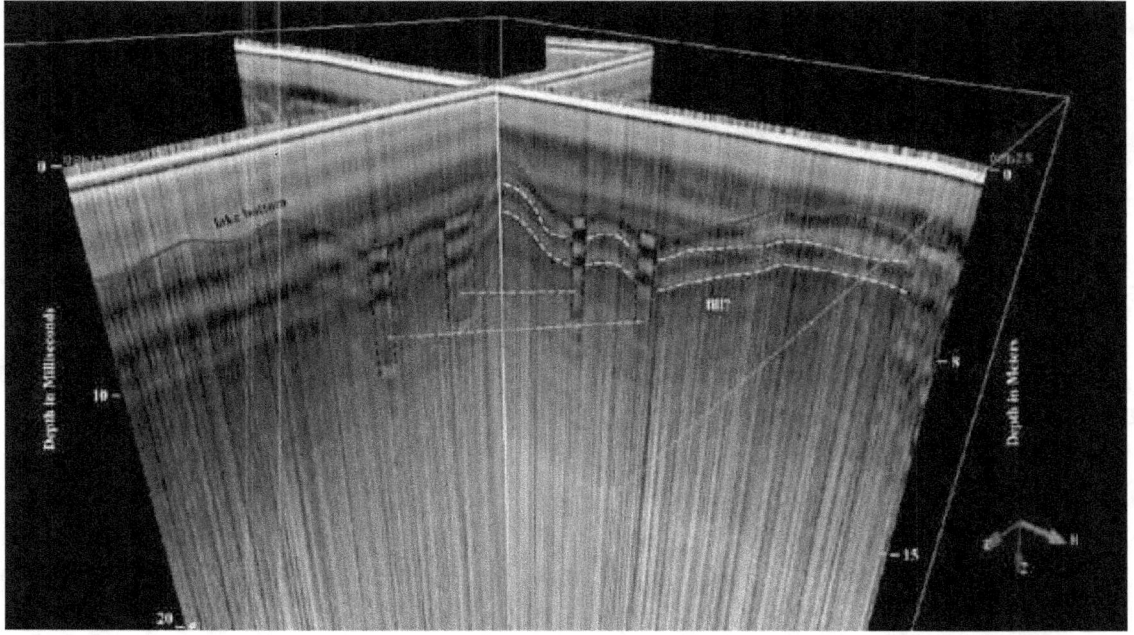

Figure 19. Seismic profiles (08b17 and 08b25) collected in Cherry Lake. Locations of lines 08b17 and 08b25 are shown in figure 17. Dashed lines represent features present in the subbottom.

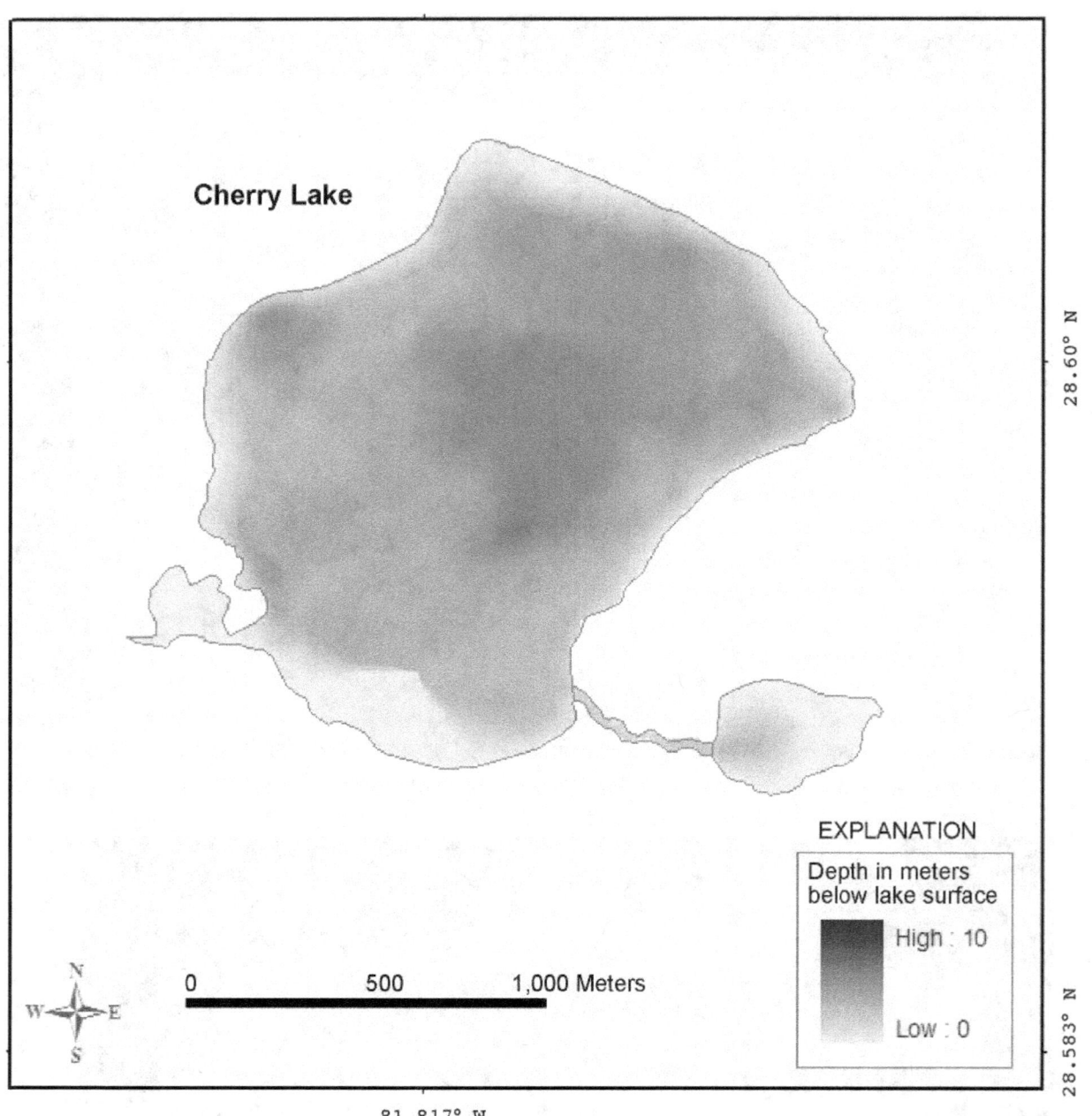

Figure 20. Bathymetric map of Cherry Lake, interpreted from seismic profiles. Refer to figure 17 for trackline coverage since not all of the lake was surveyed.

Continuous Resistivity Profiles

Approximately 8 line-km of resistivity were collected in Cherry Lake, of which 6.2 line-km are shown as six resistivity profiles (appendix, pages A7-A13; fig. 21). The resistivity profiles show a very heterogeneous matrix below the lake. Isolated zones of low resistivity (~20-70 ohm-m) are interspersed with higher resistivity areas (~200-500 ohm-m) (fig. 22). The blue tones (low resistiv-

22

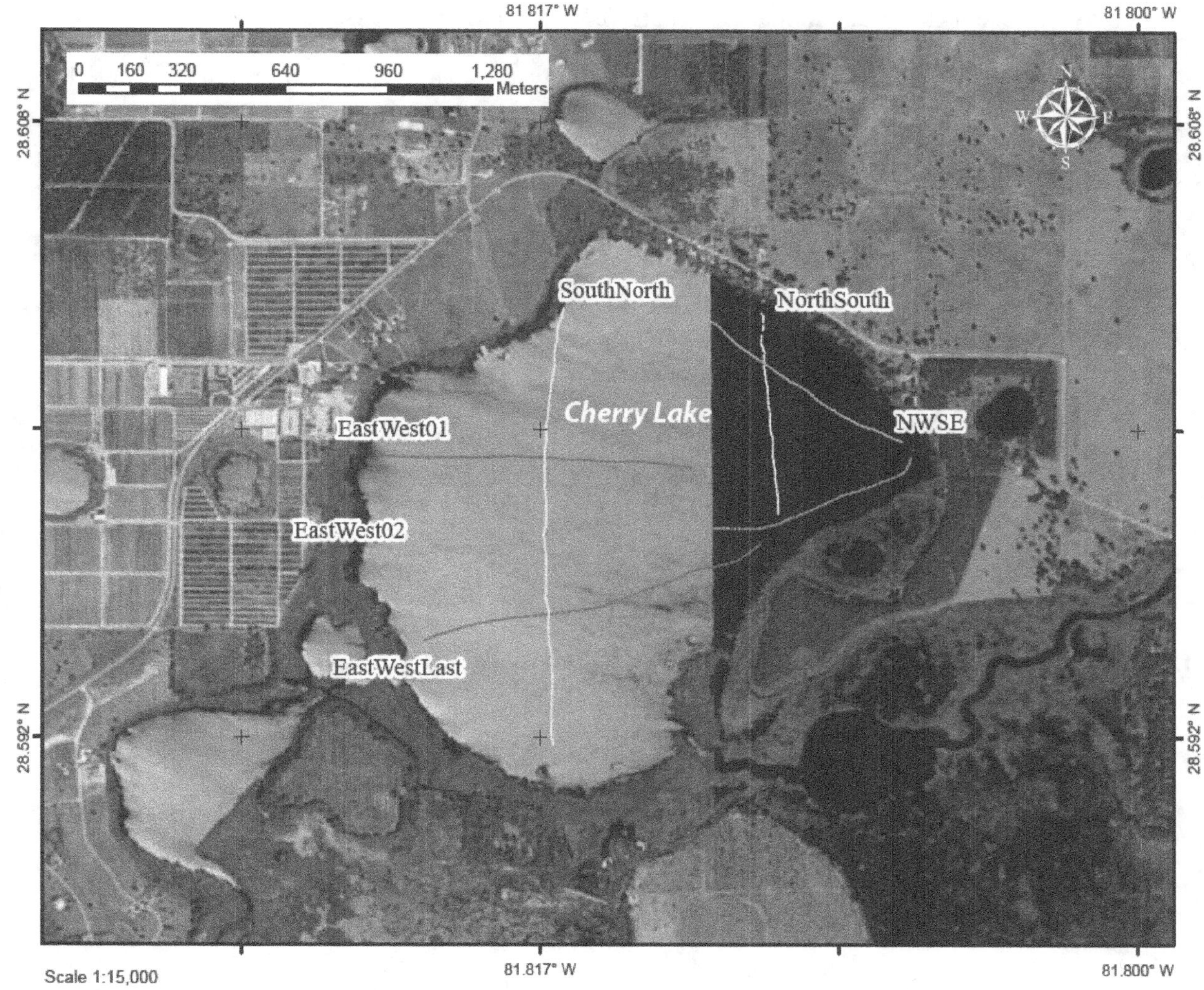

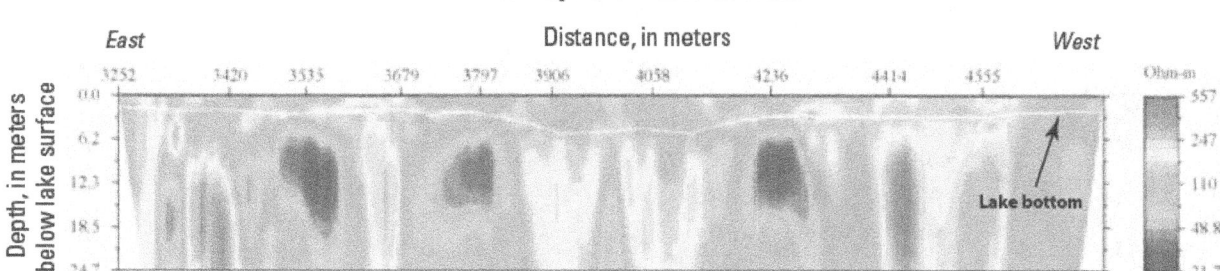

Figure 21. Map shows continuous resistivity profile tracklines in Cherry Lake.

Cherry Lake–East-West02

Figure 22. Resistivity profile (EastWest_02) shows heterogeneity in the subsurface of Cherry Lake. Ohm-m, ohm meters.

ity) may represent clay units that are extensive enough that they assist in maintaining a tight seal and low vertical hydraulic conductivity to maintain water levels in the lake. Smaller isolated zones of higher resistivity may indicate sand units that contain lesser amounts of clay and silt particles, yet maintain a low hydraulic conductivity.

Lake Colby

Seismic Profiles

Lake Colby is located in Volusia County. Extreme low-water levels in Lake Colby have left most of the lake bottom exposed. When surveying took place, the water level in the lake was much lower than shown in figure 23. At the time of this survey, three separate parts of the lake contained

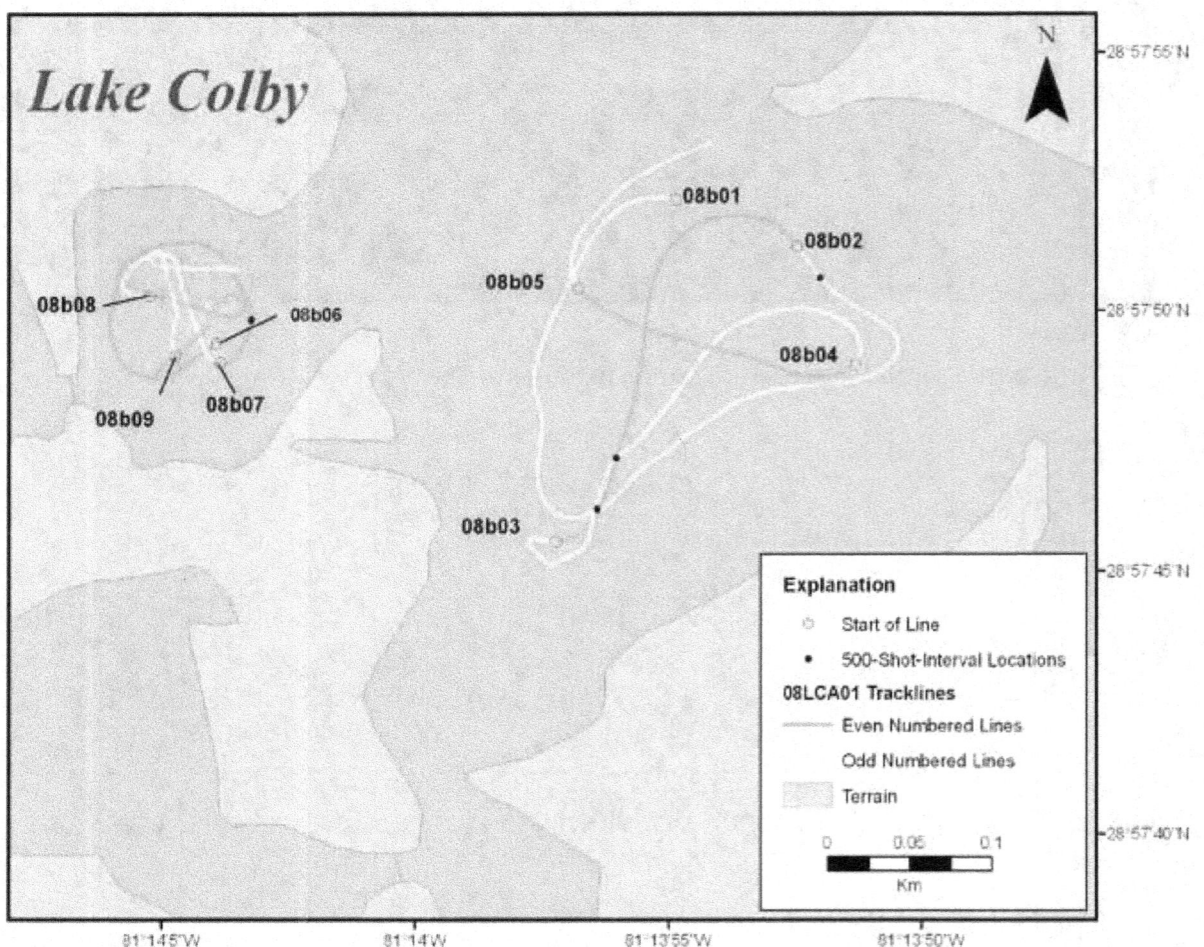

Figure 23. Seismic-profile tracklines collected in Lake Colby. The water level in the lake was much lower than shown and only two parts were accessible.

24

water: two depressions in the eastern part of the lake and an obvious 10-m-deep sinkhole-filled depression on the western edge. The seismic-profile system was able to assess one of the eastern depressions and the westernmost sinkhole-filled body of water (fig. 23). Bathymetry for Lake Colby is shown in figure 24. Two small-scale dips in the lake-bottom seismic reflectors from the eastern portion of the lake may also be seen within the subsurface (fig. 25). Other than these two

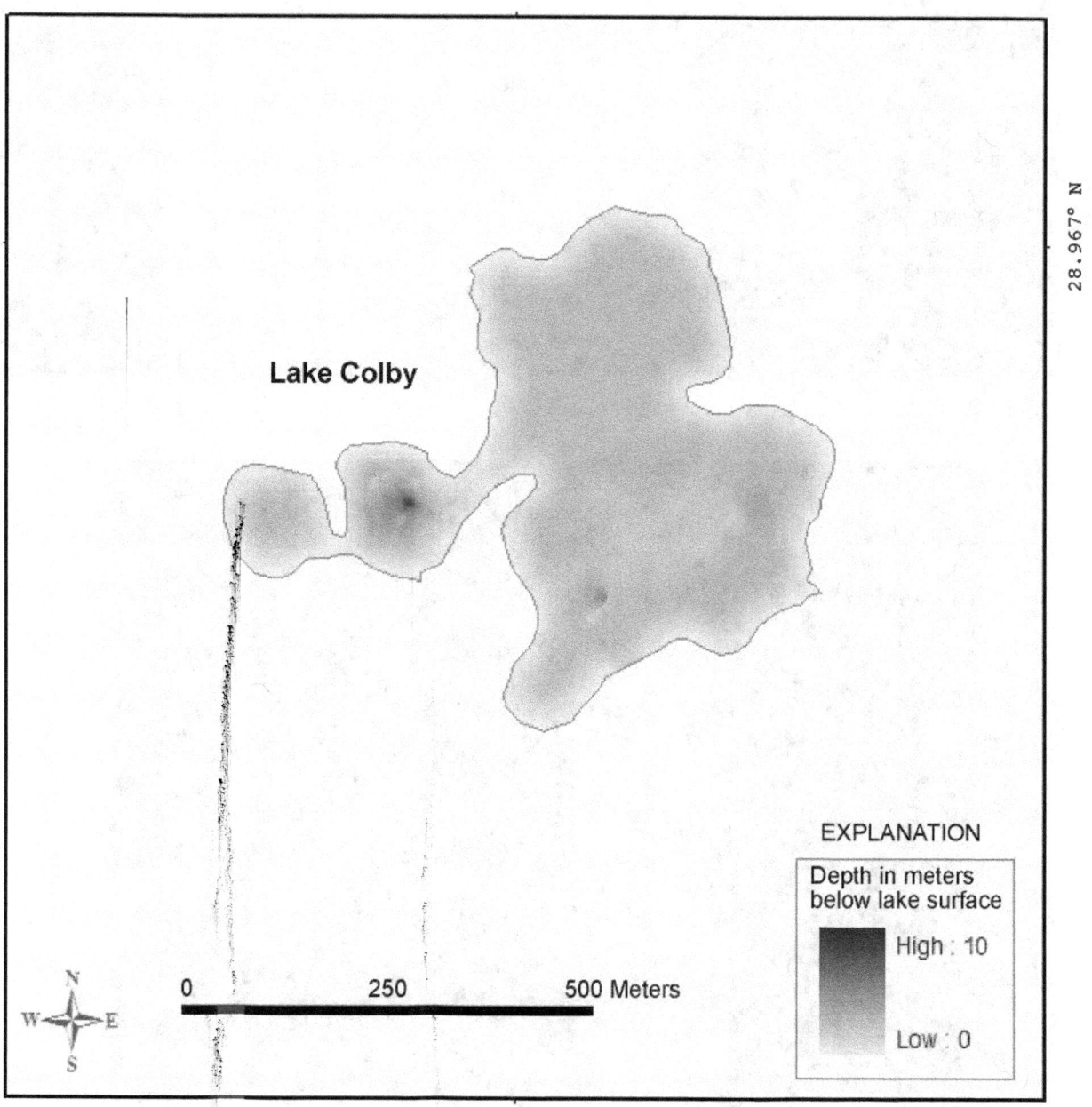

Figure 24. Bathymetric map of the lake bottom, Lake Colby, interpreted from seismic profiles. Refer to figure 23 for trackline coverage because not all of the lake was surveyed.

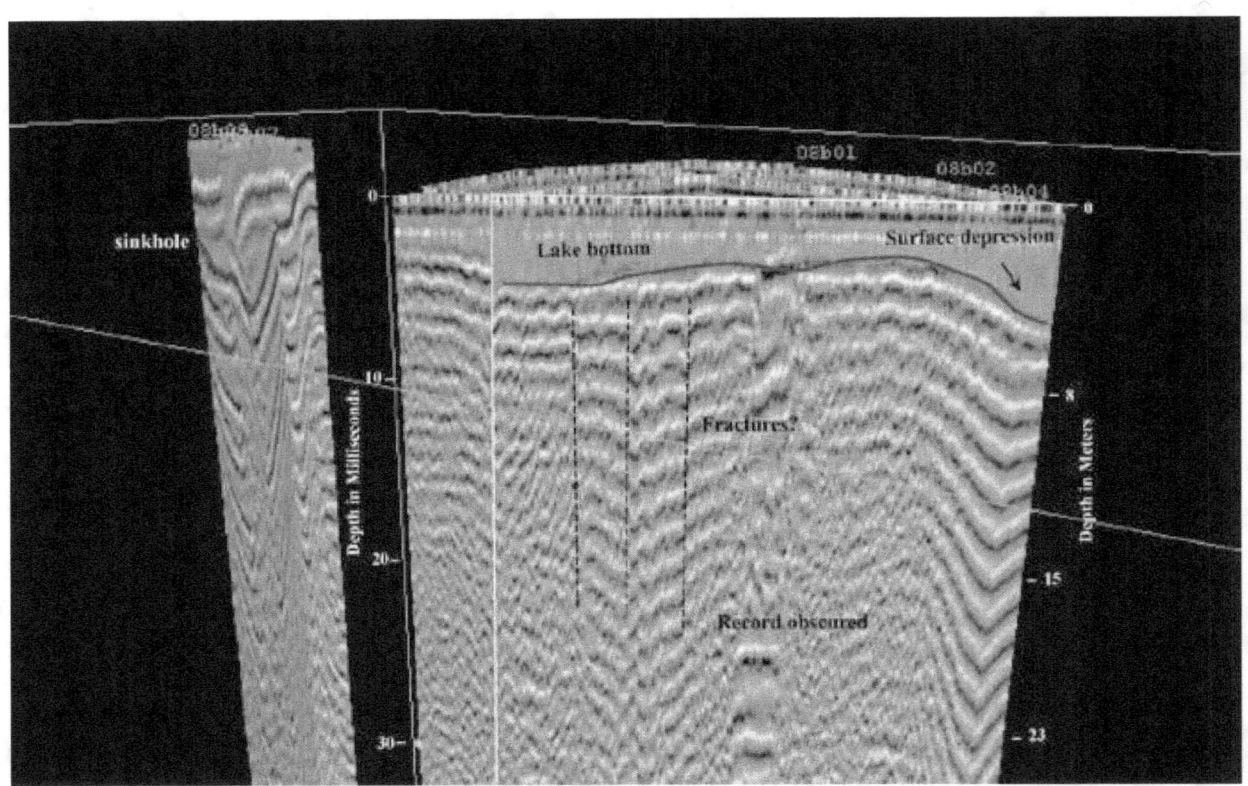

Figure 25. Seismic profile (08b04) collected in Lake Colby.

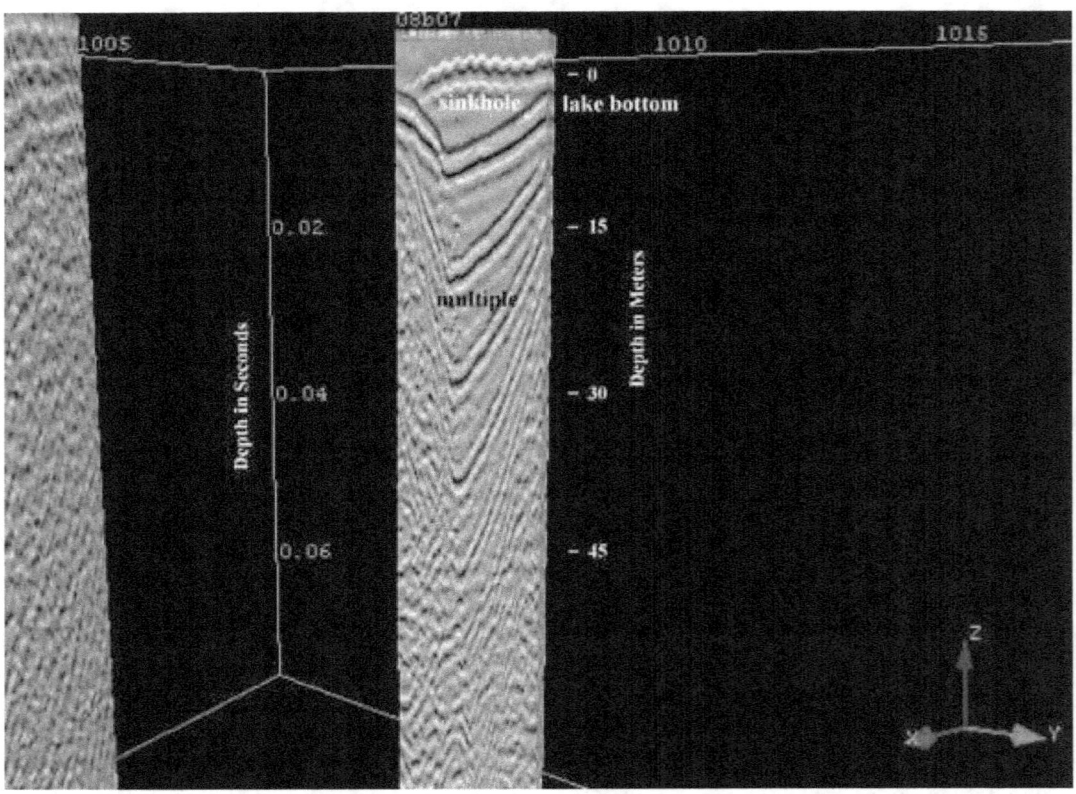

Figure 26. Seismic profile (08b07) of sinkhole in Lake Colby.

features, most of the record from this part of Lake Colby was obscured. The sinkhole located in the western portion of the lake is well defined in seismic profile as a pronounced concave reflector (fig. 26). Multiples from this reflector obscure the profile at depth, so that subsurface features associated with the sinkhole are not readily apparent.

Land-based Stationary Resistivity Profiles

Because of low water levels, two separate portions of Lake Colby were surveyed using the land-based resistivity system (fig. 27; appendix, pages A14-A16). A small, circular lake west of the main lake, ~80 m in diameter, was investigated by laying the 112-m-long cable across the small lake in an east-west and north-south transect (lines 1 and 2). Lines 1 and 2 show that the shallow subsur-

Figure 27. Lake Colby and position of land-based resistivity lines. Numbers represent the line number; green dot represents first electrode (0 m) and red dot represents last electrode (112 m).

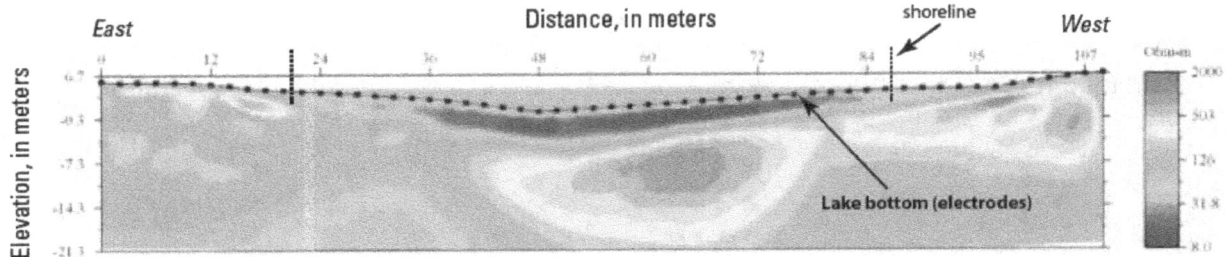

Figure 28. Land-based resistivity profile (line 1) in the small sinkhole-filled lake at Lake Colby. Note low-resistivity unit along lake bottom that may correlate to detrital organic-rich material. Ohm-m, ohm meters.

face in the deepest part of the lake is composed of conductive (low-resistivity) sediments that most likely represent organic-rich material (fig. 28; appendix, page A15). Below the low-resistivity unit is a high-resistivity body (400-800 ohm-m) that most likely represents a quartz-sand unit. This unit appears to be situated in a depression that looks similar to a subsidence-sinkhole formation. Lower-resistivity units (~10-30 ohm-m) along the edges and below the high-resistivity body are most likely composed of silty sands or clays.

Three other lines were run along the northern edge of the southern lobe of Lake Colby. Lines 3 and 4 were run at ~90 degrees from each other, and line 5 was run in an exposed muddy swale. Lines 3 and 4 show that a thin, highly resistive material (sand) occurs just below the lake bottom and a slightly more conductive material (silty sand) occurs underneath (appendix, page A16). There does not appear to be any karst sinkhole-type features in the resistivity profiles collected. The profile from line 5 indicates that below a thin and discontinuous resistive unit lies a continuous and thick (up to 13 m) conductive unit (72 ohm-m) that most likely represents a clay unit. This subsurface impermeable clay is the probable cause for the swale to remain continually wet. All resistivity profiles can be found in the Appendix.

Crooked Lake

Land-based Stationary Resistivity Profiles

Crooked Lake is located in a highly developed area of Orange County. Water levels in Crooked Lake were low at the time of this survey, approximately 1 m lower than shown in figure 29. A small, circular, sinkhole-shaped pond was surveyed on the northern side of Crooked Lake, and two lines were surveyed in the southern arm of the lake (appendix, pages A17-A19). Resistivity data (lines Crooked 01 through 03) collected in the small, circular pond indicate a broad, structural subsidence-type sinkhole formation (fig. 30; appendix, page A18). The structure contains high-resistivity material (~500 ohm-m) that is most likely indicative of quartz sand. There also appears to

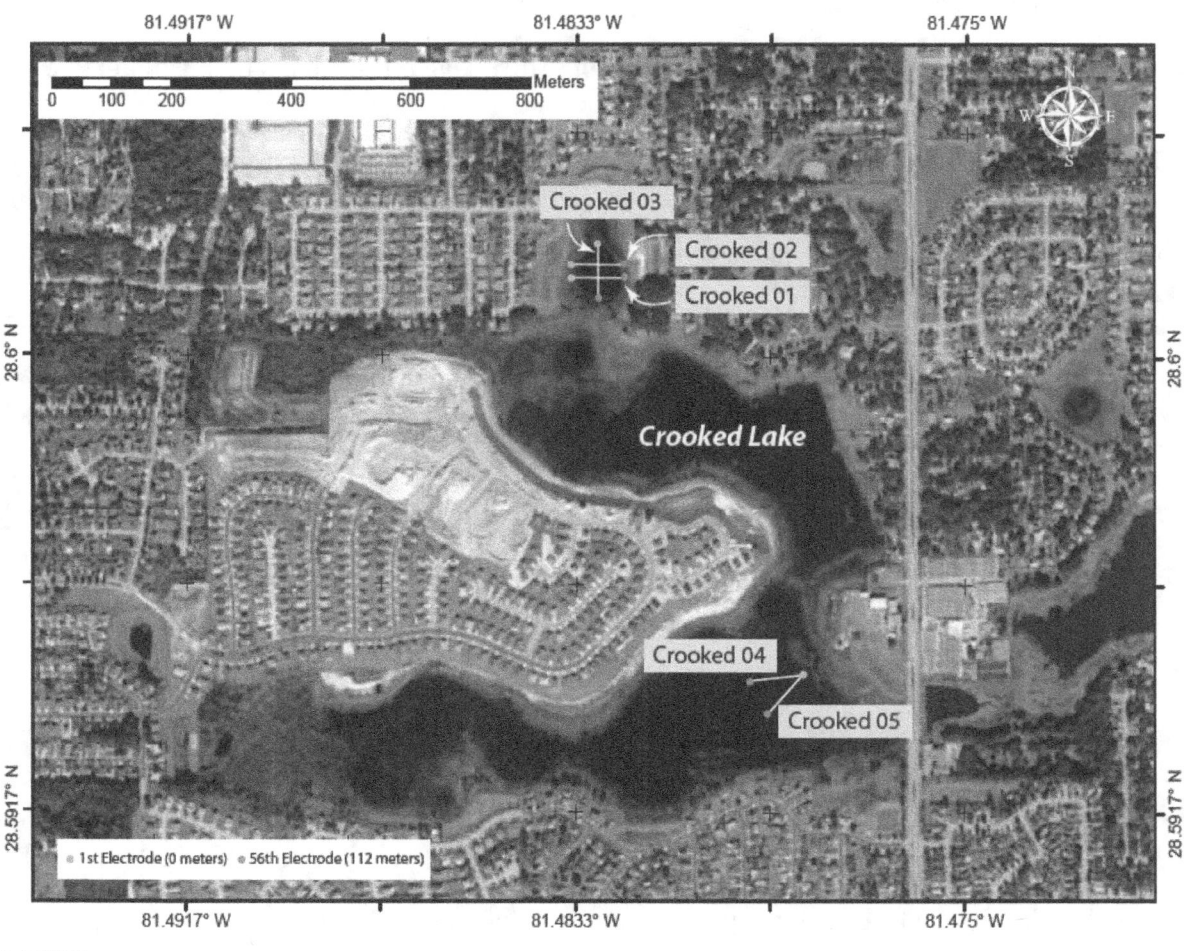

Scale 1:10,000

Figure 29. Map shows the position of stationary resistivity lines in Crooked Lake. Numbers represent the line number; green dot represents first electrode (0 m) and red dot represents last electrode (112 m).

Crooked Lake–Line 01

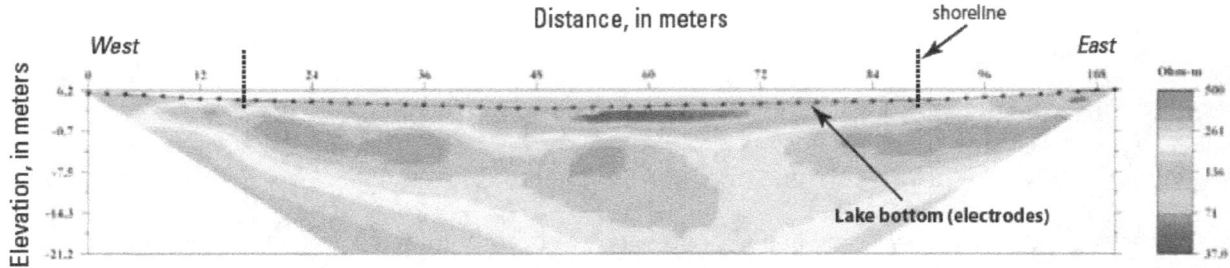

Figure 30. Resistivity profile (Crooked 01) shows broad subsidence-sinkhole structure, Crooked Lake. Ohm-m, ohm meters.

be a thin conductive (low-resistivity) unit in the center of the lake that could be the result of organic material deposition.

The two lines (Crooked 04 and 05) in the southern arm of Crooked Lake look very different than the small, circular feature to the north (appendix, page A19). Line 04 ran parallel to a dry ridge, at the time of surveying, in a very shallow section of the lake (<0.3 m). There appears to be a sand unit overlying a silty sand or clay unit. The resistivity profile along line 04 shows a more continuous sand unit, most likely an extension of the sand ridge to the north of the line, and a more conductive unit below at a depth of ~10 m near the center of the profile. Line 05 was run from the northeast to the southwest into the lake; however, the water depth did not change from near the shore out to the end of the cable. Results from line 05 show that the sand body in the shallow subsurface pinches out at ~40 m from shore, and the remaining unit consists of a low-resistivity unit most likely composed of silty sands or clays.

Lake Helen

Seismic Profiles

Lake Helen is located in Volusia County, is long (~900 m), narrow (70-200 m), and bifurcated. Lake Helen occupies the lower elevations of the sand hills within the Central Lakes District (Kindinger and others, 2000). The elongate shape of the lake would indicate a collection of small sinkholes joined by a dissolution valley. However, seismic profiles indicate a single, large subsur-

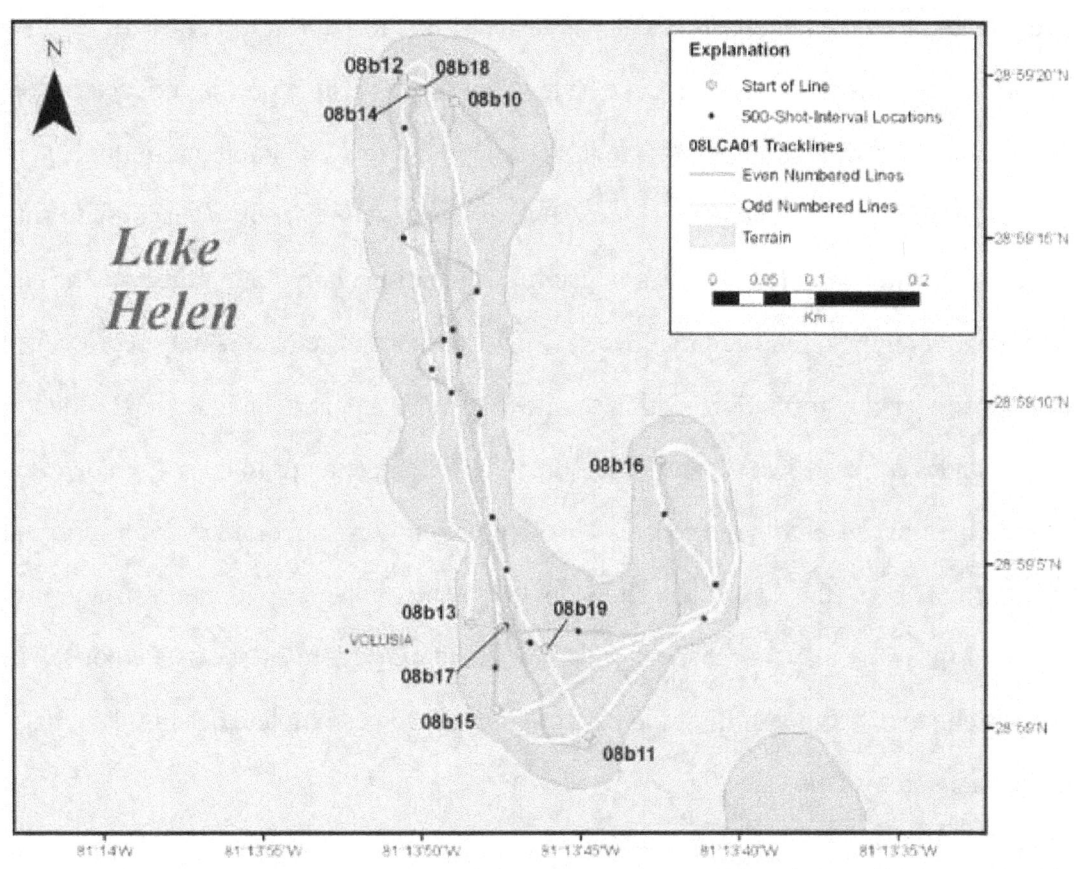

Figure 31. Seismic-profile tracklines collected in Lake Helen.

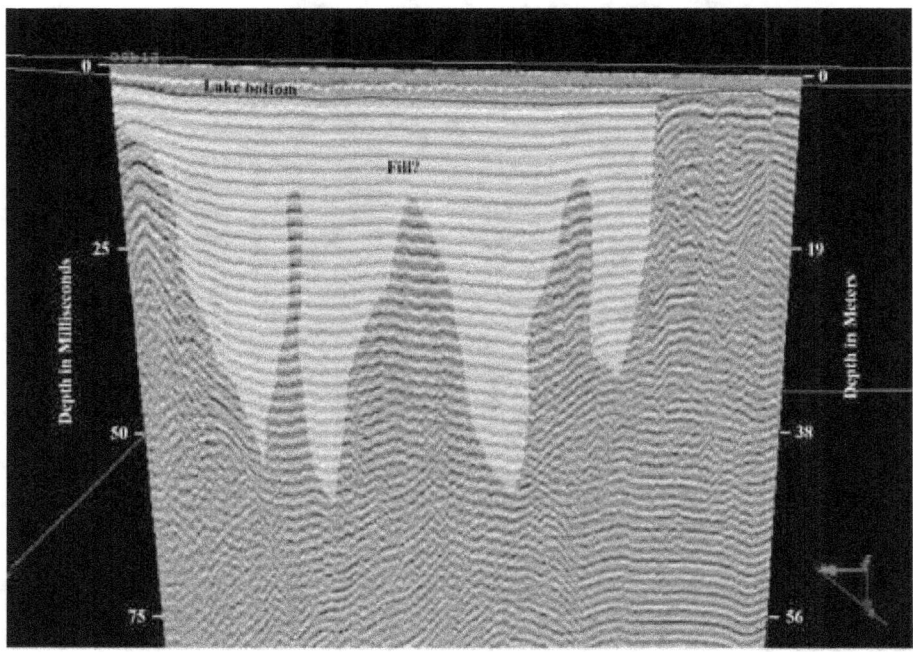

Figure 32. Seismic-profile line (08b12) collected in Lake Helen with interpretation of large fill cavities. Location of line 08b12 is shown in figure 31.

face feature extending into the underlying Ocala Limestone and Floridan Aquifer system. Figure 31 shows the seismic-profile tracklines for Lake Helen. All of the seismic profiles collected along the axis of the main leg show similar patterns to the profile in figure 32. Combining multiple seismic profiles in close proximity to each other increases confidence in the acoustic response to subsurface features. Overall, the patterns show a large area of repetitive horizontal reflectors, filling a void between higher angle, more chaotic reflectors. The latter set of reflectors may represent the Ocala Limestone or host clay formations within the Hawthorn Group, and the horizontal reflectors represent fill within a very large karst feature (fig. 32). The feature extends to over 45 m deep and contains very steep pinnacles within the center. This interpretation is supported by high-resistivity values in adjacent CRP data (fig. 33), which show possible center collapse within a resistant, low-resistivity material (possibly clay; see discussion in next section). Figure 34 shows a color-shaded relief map of this collapse feature; infill of the collapse appears to be complete because lake bathymetry is consistent across the lake (fig. 35).

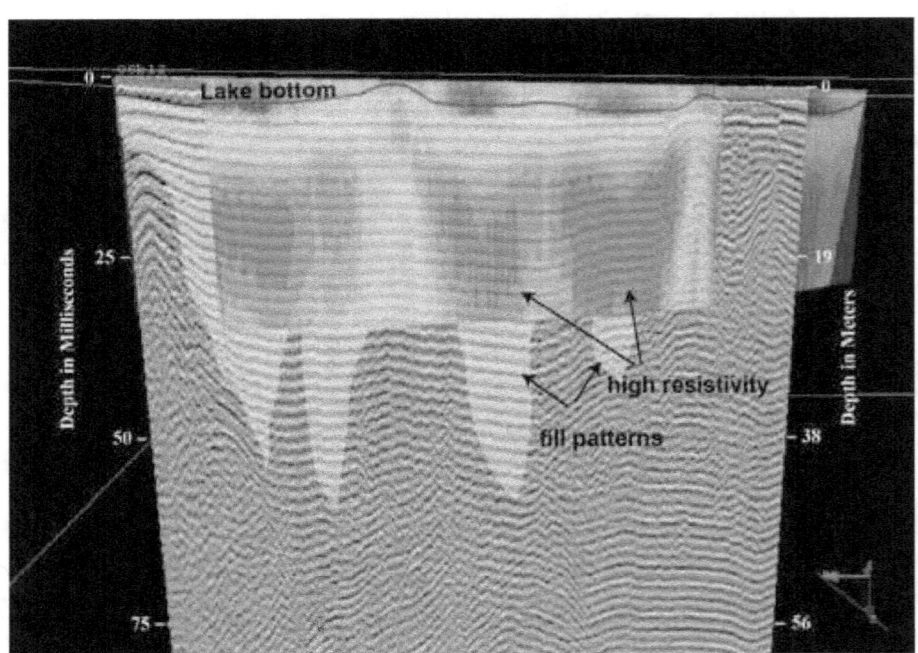

Figure 33. Seismic-profile line (08b12) with overlay of adjacent continuous resistivity profile (Helen_02). High resistivity within the resistivity profile corresponds to the area designated as fill in the seismic profile.

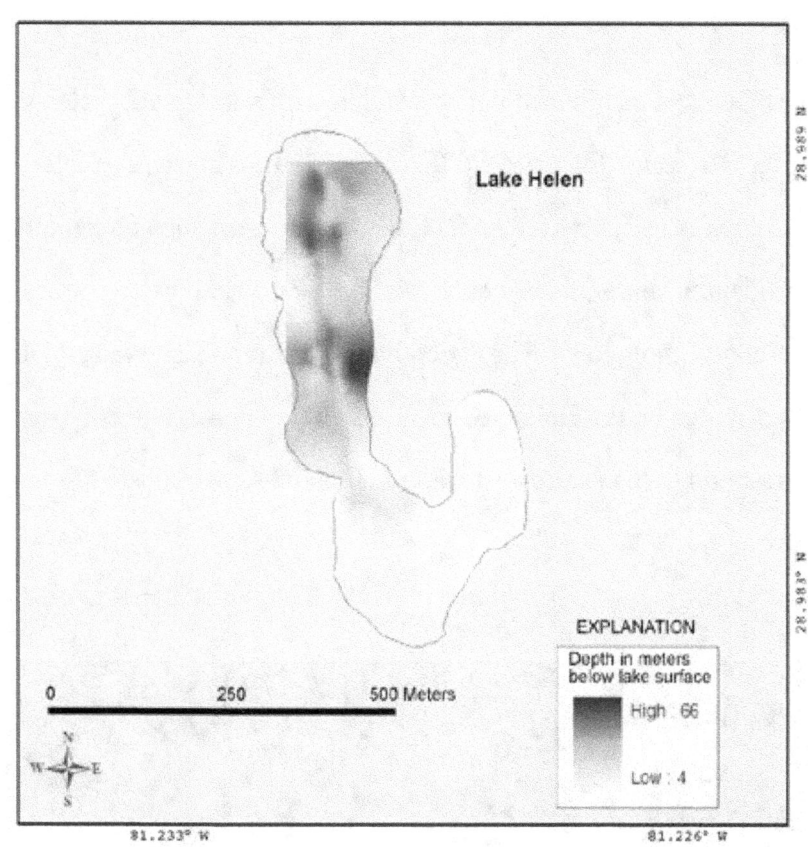

Figure 34. Color-shaded relief map of a structural horizon below Lake Helen, interpreted from seismic profiles (see base of fill polygon in figure 32).

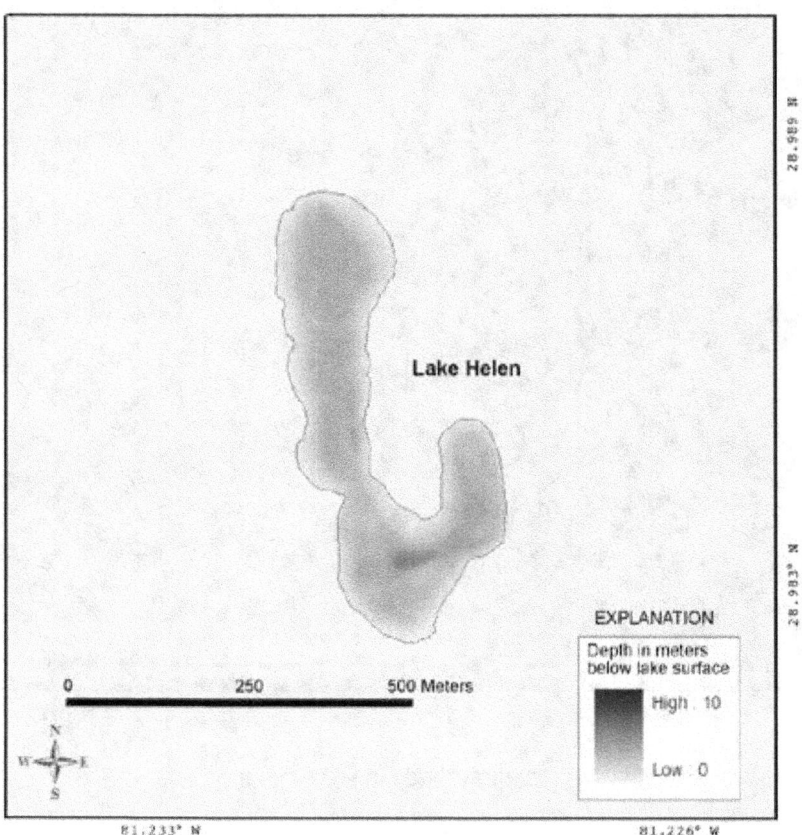

Figure 35. Bathymetric map of Lake Helen, interpreted from seismic profiles. Lake-bottom depth does not appear to be dependent on subbottom features.

33

Continuous Resistivity Profiles

Approximately 3 line-km of CRP were collected in Lake Helen with numerous overlapping lines in the main lobe of the lake (fig. 36; appendix, pages A20-A25). CRP data from line Helen_02 show that the lake consists of mostly high-resistivity materials (200-400 ohm-m) such as sand that may indicate subsidence and subsequent infilling of surficial sands (fig. 37). There are two areas that indicate that more conductive (clay) lithologies occur at depth and may represent edges of a sinkhole (at ~700 m and ~1,000 m distance on the Helen_02 profile). The low resistivities observed directly above these two areas correspond to the shallowest water depth and may indicate the rim of a sinkhole.

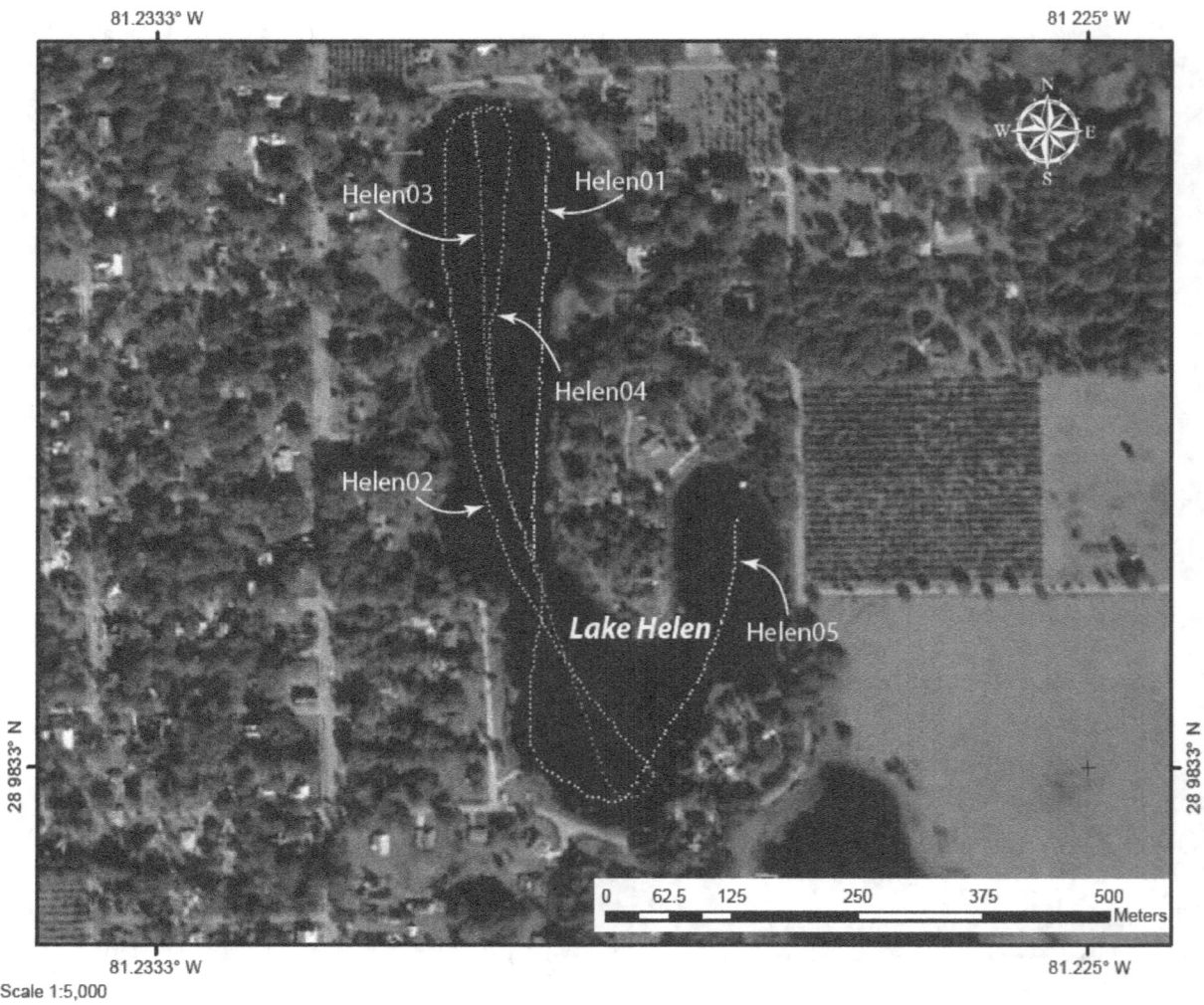

Figure 36. Map shows location of continuous resistivity profile tracklines in Lake Helen.

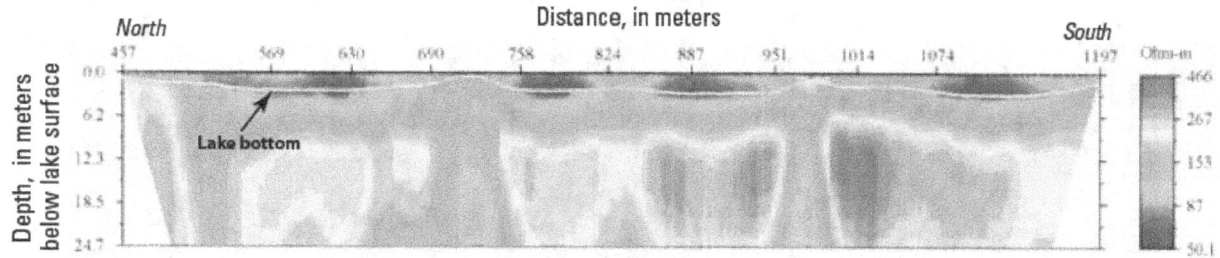

Figure 37. Continuous resistivity profile (Helen_02) along the main lobe of Lake Helen. Profile shows high-resistivity units (sand) separated by narrow low-resistivity bodies (clay?) and may indicate subsidence from deep-sinkhole formation. Ohm-m, ohm meters.

The short eastern lobe of Lake Helen appears to be a possible sinkhole feature with high-resistivity material (~600 ohm-m) in the center and a rim of low-resistivity material (~150 ohm-m) to the south (line Helen_05; appendix, page A25). There also appears to be a 2- to 4-m-thick conductive unit just below the lake bottom that may indicate a collection or accumulation of organic material that occurs between 2,800 and 2,880 m along profile.

Lake Hiawassee

Continuous Resistivity Profiles

Lake Hiawassee, located in central Orange County, is a well-developed residential lake that is used heavily by boaters and skiers. Continuous resistivity profile tracklines are shown in figure 38. CRP results indicate very sharp boundaries in resistivity throughout the lake (fig. 39; appendix, pages A26-A32). High-resistivity areas (~200 ohm-m) are very distinct and have nearly vertical "walls," indicating a very short lateral transition in lithology (fig. 39). These nearly vertical transition zones may be the result of a collapse-sinkhole formation.

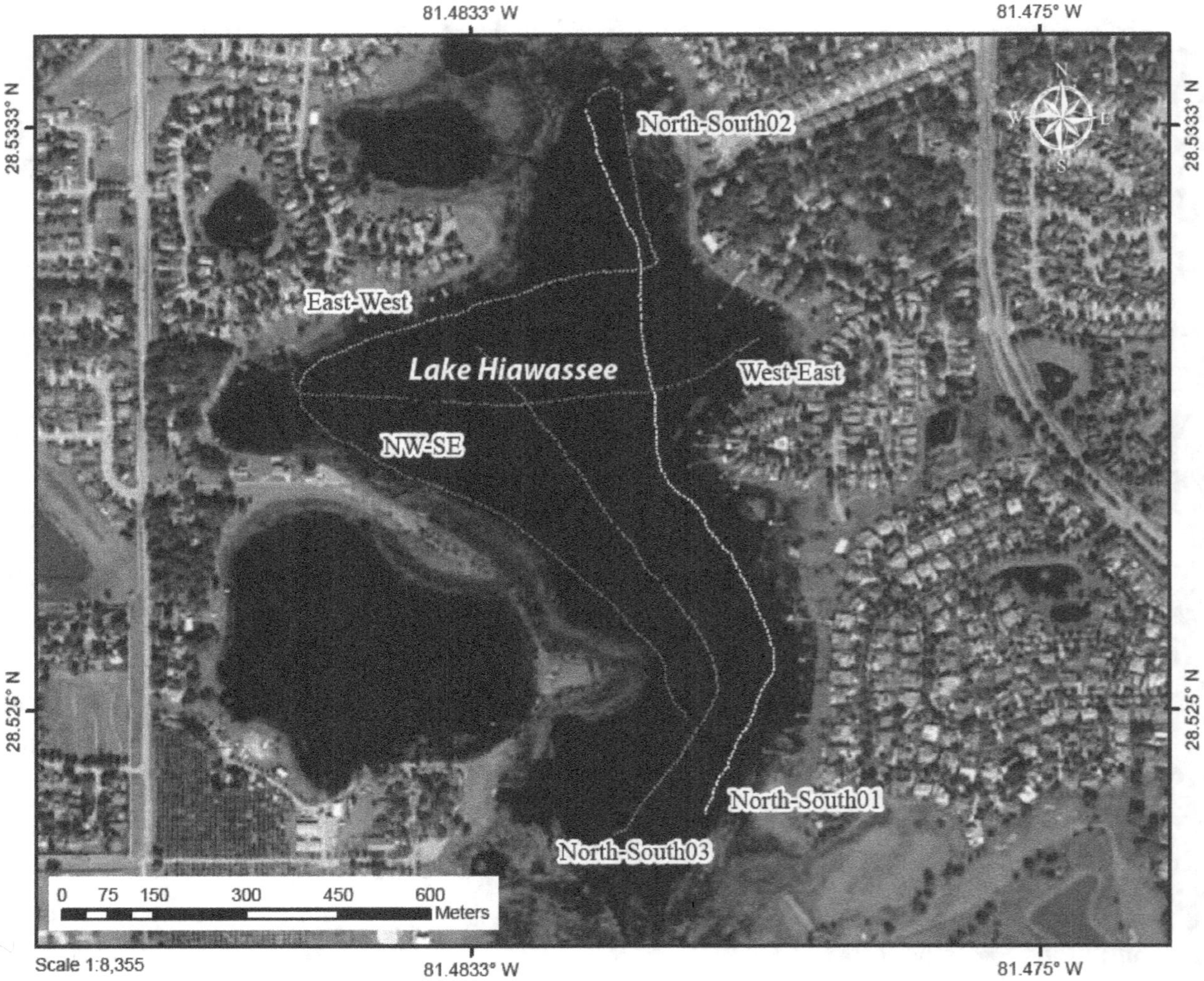

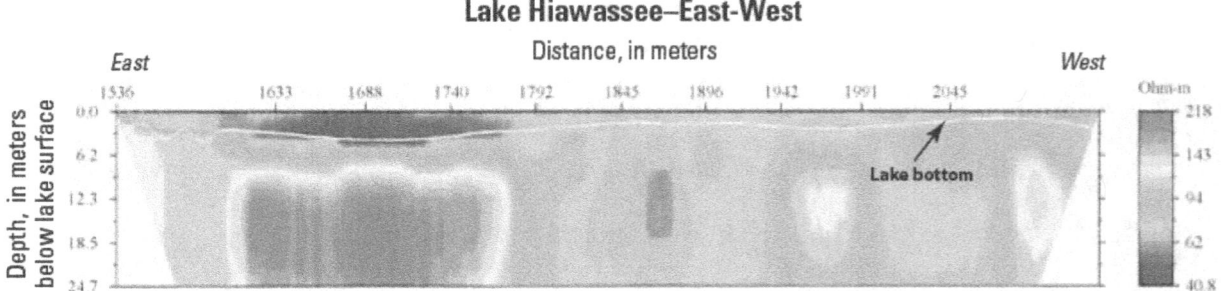

Figure 38. Map shows Continuous resistivity profile tracklines for Lake Hiawassee.

Lake Hiawassee–East-West

Figure 39. Continuous resistivity profile of east-west transect along northern section of Lake Hiawassee. Ohm-m, ohm meters.

Johns Lake

Seismic Profiles

Johns Lake is a series of interconnected shallow depressions occupying the inter-ridge areas within the Central Lakes District (fig. 2). Johns Lake is located on the border of Lake and Orange Counties south of Lake Apopka. The lake is surrounded by agricultural land but includes a residential population along the northern shore of the central and western half of the lake. Studies in this area have shown this lake configuration typically represents small individual sinkholes, joined by dissolution valleys (Kindinger and others, 2000). Forty HRSP lines were acquired across the vari-

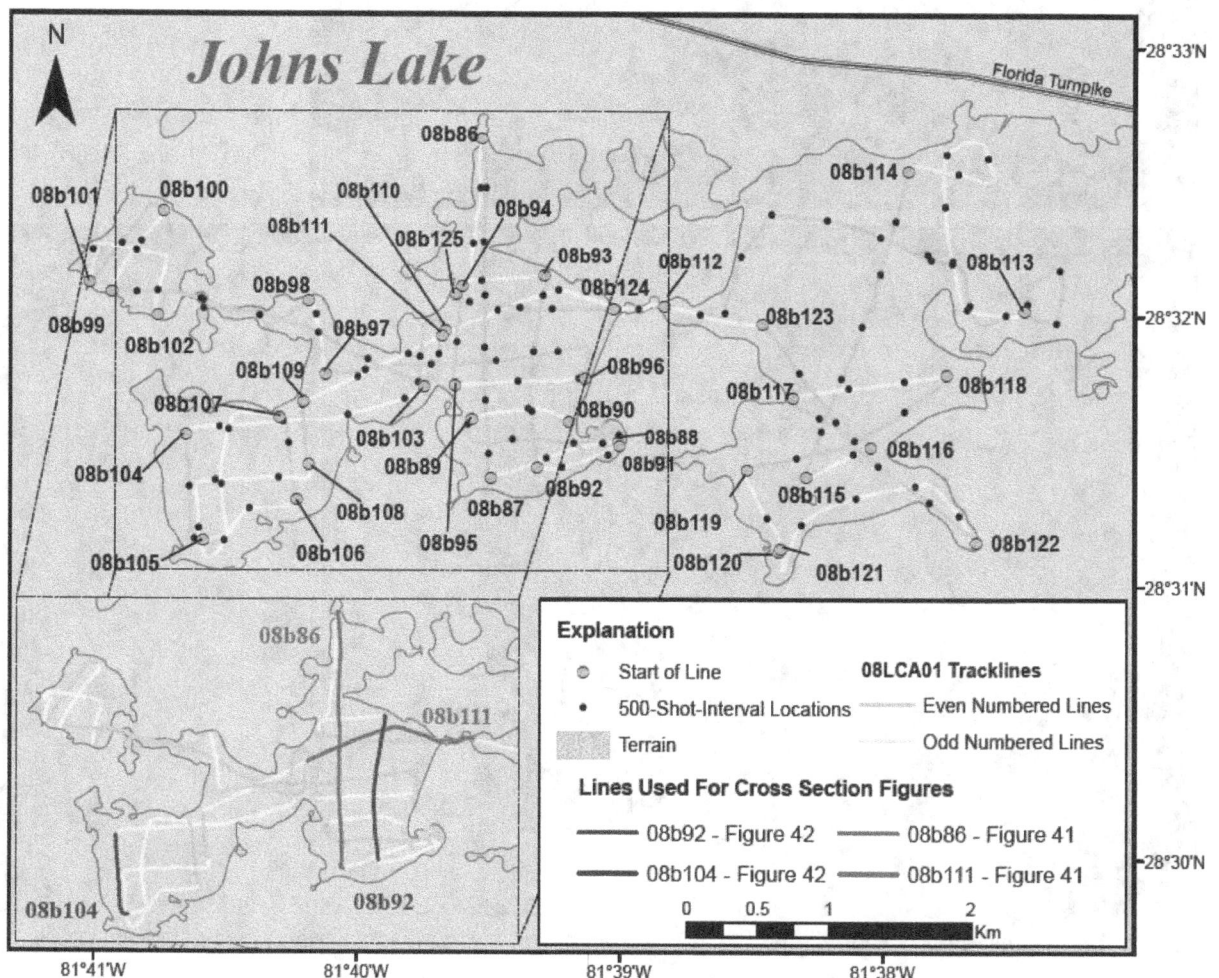

Figure 40. Seismic-profile tracklines in Johns Lake.

ous open areas of the lake (fig. 40). Seismic profiles (08b111 and 08b86) from the lake are shown in figure 41. The profile shows very little resolvable data at depth, most likely due to the shallow water depth, vegetation growing within the lake, and potential accumulation of organics and biogenic gas. Below the surface reflector, there is little cohesiveness in the acoustic signal, and the record appears to be dominated by noise. Comparison of the seismic record with the CRP shows a correlation between surface depressions and high-resistivity values at depth (fig. 42). The shallow depressions that exist at the surface may be expressions of subsurface dissolution that correlates with the expression shown in the

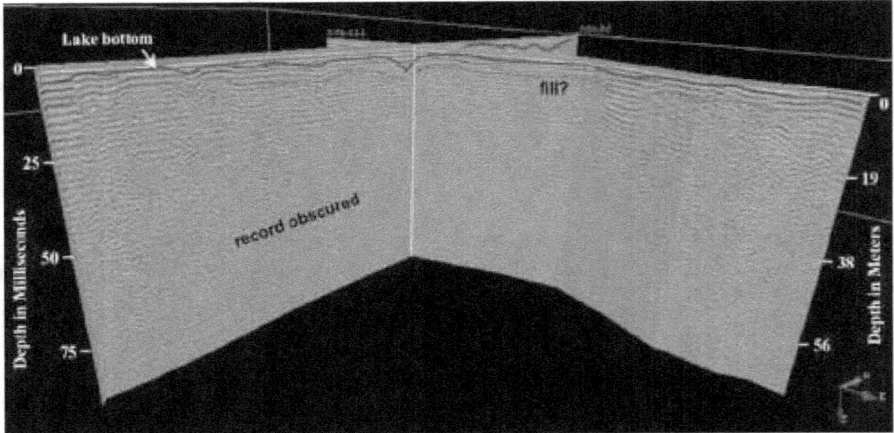

Figure 41. Seismic profiles (08b111 and 08b86) collected in Johns Lake.

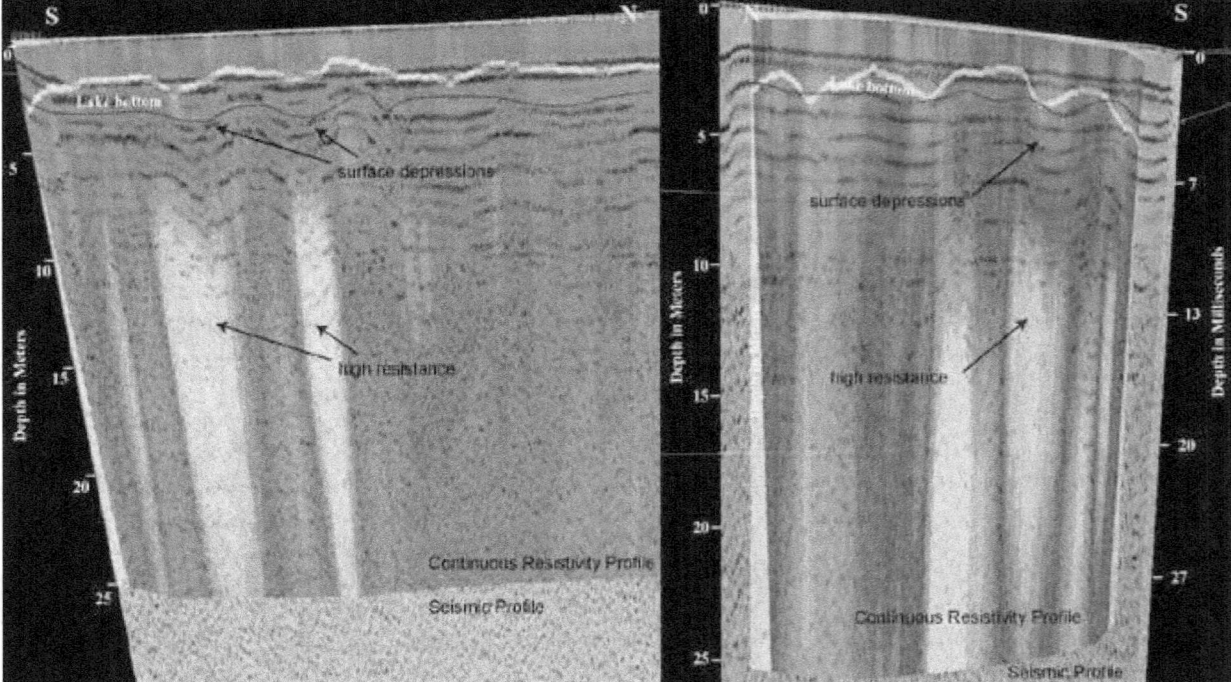

Figure 42. Seismic profiles (08b92 and 08b104) superimposed with adjacent continuous resistivity-profile lines Johns_Middle_S-N and Johns_West_S-N, respectively (color profiles). High resistivity (yellow) shown in the continuous resistivity profile section corresponds to surface depressions identified on the seismic profiles.

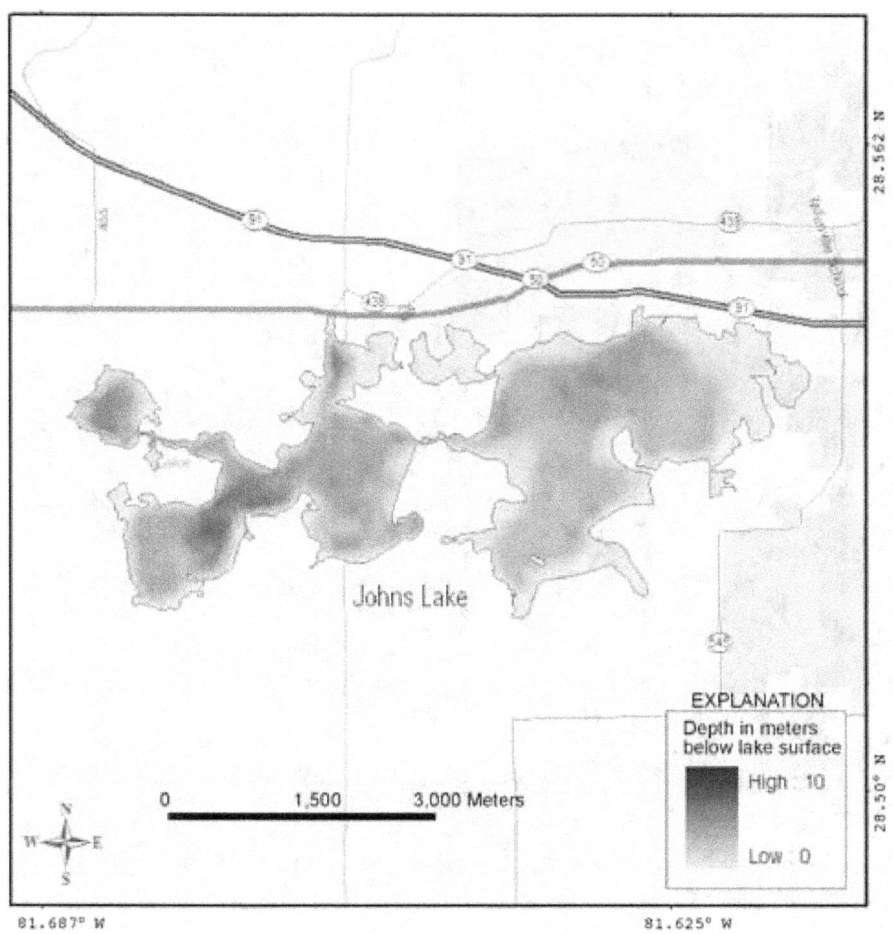

Figure 43. Bathymetric map of Johns Lake, interpreted from seismic profiles. Refer to figure 40 for trackline coverage because not all of the lake was surveyed.

CRP plots (fig. 42). A shaded-relief map of the lake bottom (determined from the seismic data) is shown in figure 43.

Continuous Resistivity Profiles

Johns Lake is a large lake with multiple lobes/sections. The lake will thus be divided into four areas for discussion: northwest, west, middle, and east lakes (fig. 44; appendix, pages A33-A65).

The northwest portion of Johns Lake is small, and ~1.4 line-km of resistivity data were collected. Isolated areas of high-resistivity materials in the subsurface were observed in the north-

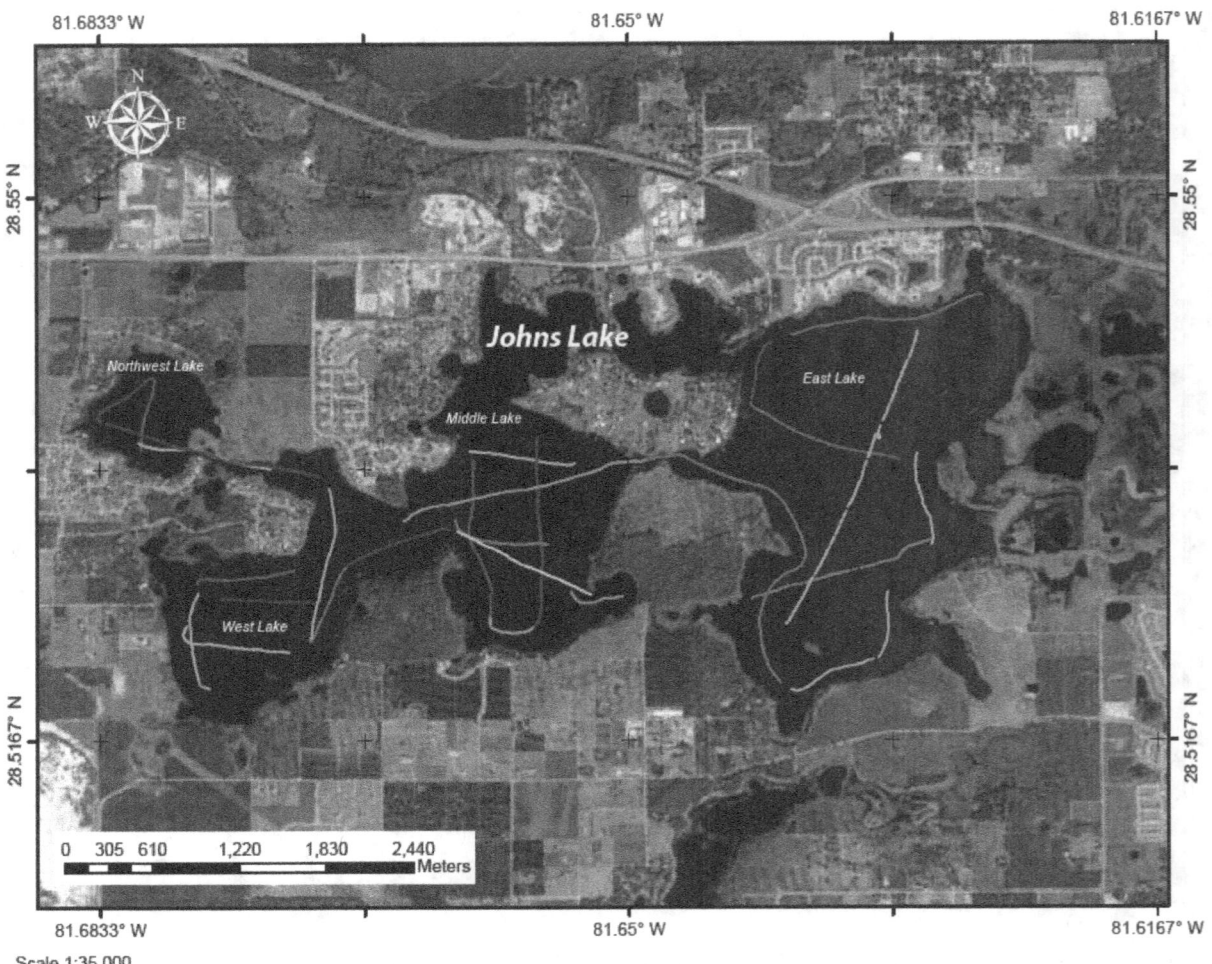

Figure 44. Continuous resistivity profile lines in the four areas of Johns Lake.

south profile (appendix, pages A34-A36). This could represent fingering of sands and clays either along vertical karst features or other heterogeneities in the original deposition of the sediments. The transect through the channel from the northwest lake to west lake (appendix, page A36) shows very little structure. It is believed that the changes in resistivity between 400 and 555 m (distance along profile) represent noise created during the transit of the cable through reeds.

A total of 7.3 line-km of CRP was collected in the western portion of Johns Lake. CRP data show a variable subsurface structure with areas of high (~300 ohm-m) and low resistivity (~35 ohm-m; fig. 45; appendix, pages A37-A44). The variability seen here is similar to that described in the north-south profile in northwest lake. There are discrete areas of high-resistivity materials sur-rounded by low-resistivity materials over relatively short distances. The high-resistivity areas may

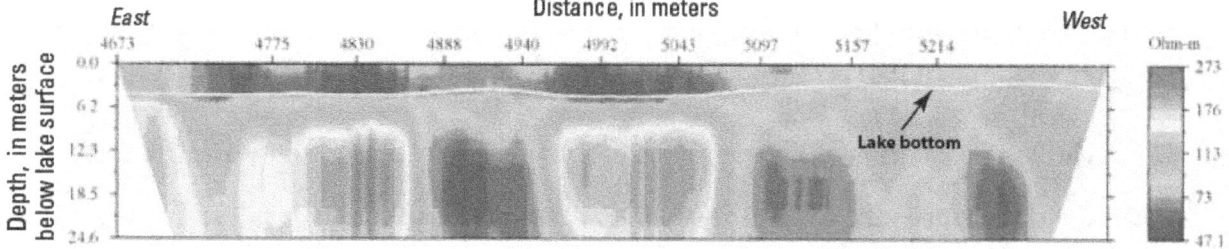

Johns Lake–West_E-W

Figure 45. Resistivity profile of western lake region of Johns Lake shows areas of high- and low-resistivity materials (West_E-W profile). Ohm-m, ohm meters.

represent ravel zones as a result of dissolution and subsidence of deep underlying limestone surface and subsequent infilling of overlying quartz sand.

Approximately 6.9 line-km of resistivity data were collected in the middle portion of Johns Lake (appendix, pages A45-A54). The Johns_Middle _N-S profile contains several shifts in the measured resistivity data (appendix, page A51). These shifts create noise in the data and are difficult to remove; therefore, the data in the vicinity of the shifts are blanked out. There are other areas in the middle lake area that may indicate lithologic changes due to sinkhole formation. The profile from Johns_Middle_smallSEfeature (appendix, page A52) shows low resistivity (~54 ohm-m) and possible subsidence in the southeast corner near the small, circular feature. Another 'typical' sinkhole/subsidence feature with low resistivity flanked by high resistivity occurs near the southern shore of the middle lake as shown in the Johns_Middle_SW-E profile (appendix, page A49). A tran-

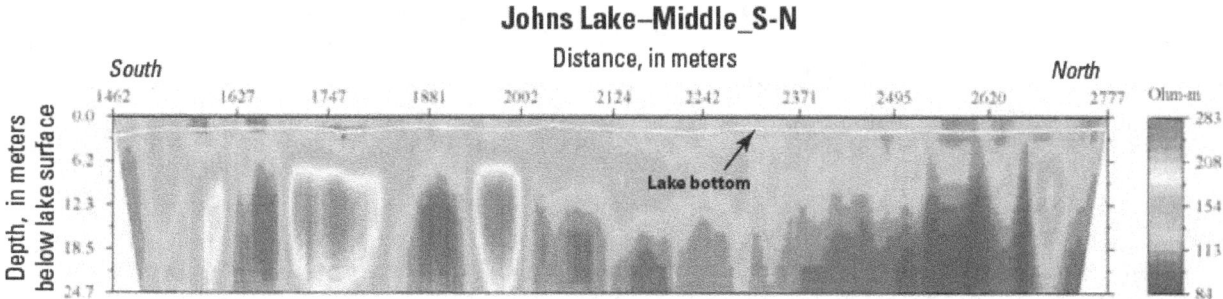

Johns Lake–Middle_S-N

Figure 46. Resistivity profile of Johns_Middle_S-N shows isolated high-resistivity areas in the southern section and a transition into a broad low-resistivity area. Ohm-m, ohm meters.

sition of isolated high-resistivity units into a low-resistivity subbottom can be seen on the Johns_ Middle_S-N profile in the middle lake (fig. 46). This transition may represent a series of multiple (clustered) infilled sinkholes in a broad, stable area beneath the lake.

The east lake portion is the largest area surveyed in Johns Lake with ~10 km of resistivity data collected (appendix, pages A55-A65). Patterns in resistivity data observed in the east lake

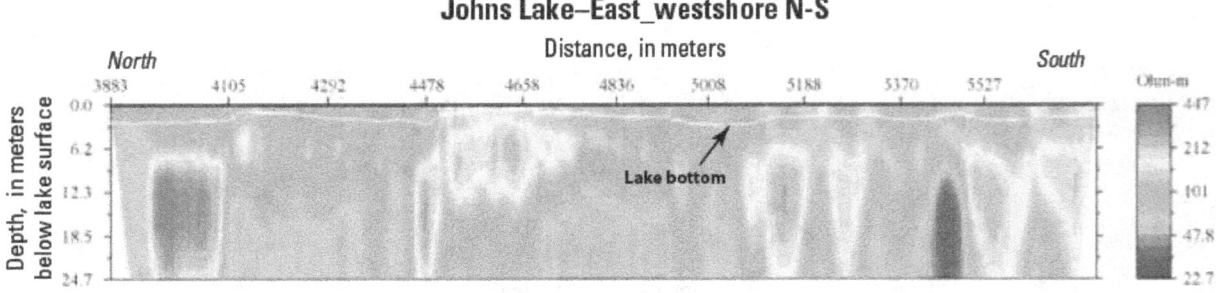

Figure 47. Resistivity profile of Johns_East_westshore_N-S collected in the east lake portion of Johns Lake. Ohm-m, ohm meters.

area are similar to those observed in the other portions of Johns Lake. There appears to be a slight increase in the number of high-resistivity areas (fig. 47) that may indicate an increase in the spatial distribution and occurrence of karst development.

Lake Louisa

Continuous Resistivity Profiles

Lake Louisa, located in Lake County, is large, oval in shape, and has an approximate diameter of 3.5 km. Approximately 25 line-km of continuous resistivity were run along the north-south and east-west transects (appendix, pages A66-A74). Figure 48 shows the tracklines of CRP and their spatial extent within the lake. The individual resistivity profiles are long and tend to be compressed when compared to smaller lakes surveyed in this study. Resistivity profiles show a very heterogeneous subbottom. Data appear chaotic at times and are difficult to interpret and extract the difference between karst or other geologic features and inherent noise. Nonetheless, there is an area of

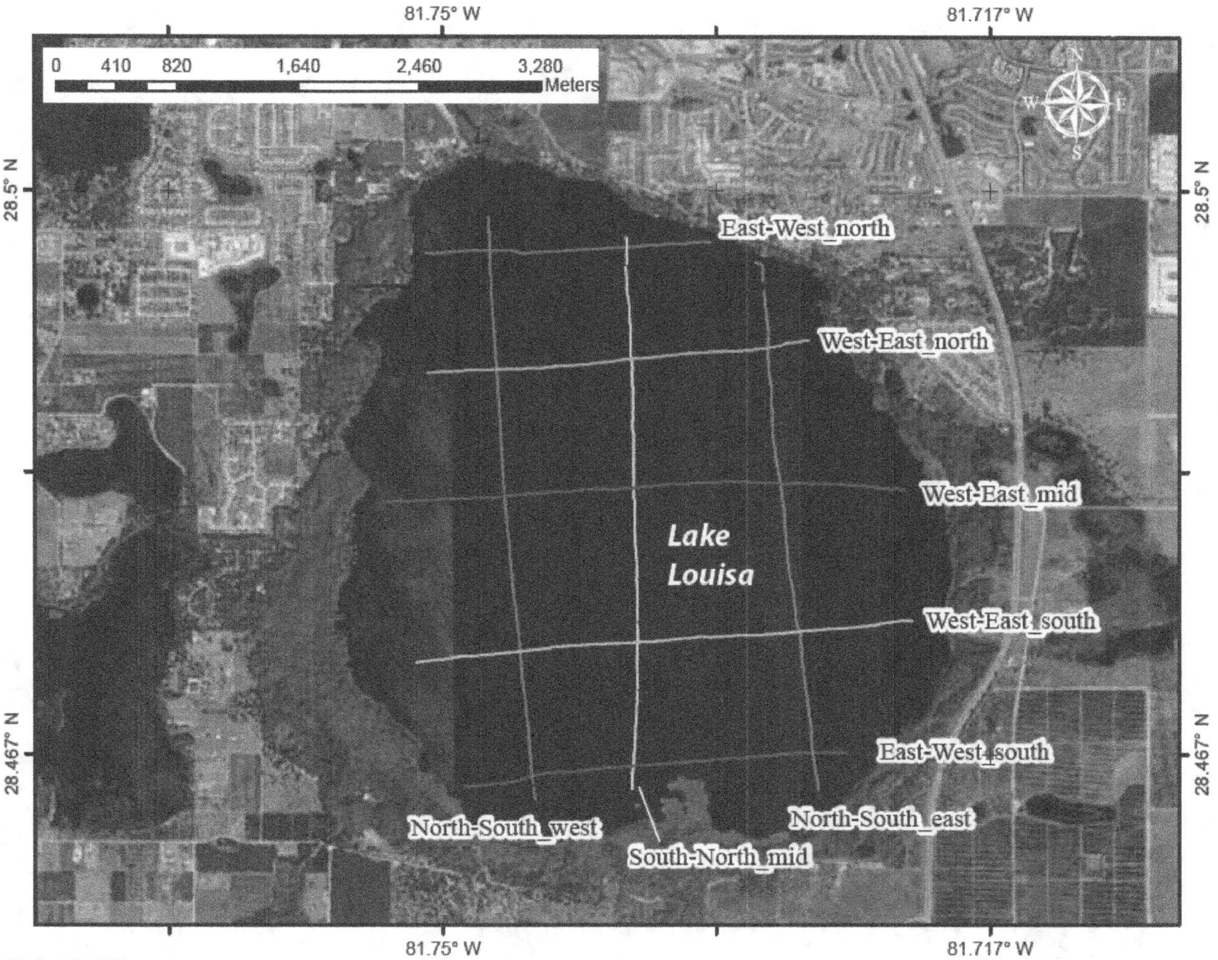

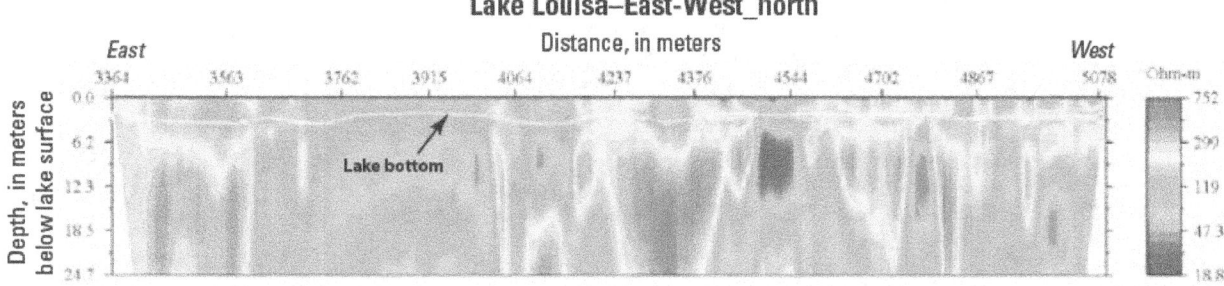

Figure 48. Map shows the location of continuous resistivity profile tracklines in Lake Louisa.

interest along the Louisa_East-West_north transect (fig. 49) between 4,200 and 4,450 m. This area could be interpreted as a structural depression that infilled with resistive sands, although structural information, such as high-resolution seismic profiling, would be needed to confirm this idea. Isolat-

Figure 49. Continuous resistivity profile (east-west_north line) in Lake Louisa along the northern shore shows the spatial variability in resistivity. Ohm-m, ohm meters.

ed areas of low-resistivity materials occur in several of the profiles. The low-resistivity areas occur at similar depths between 6 and 13 m below the water surface. However, some are deeper (appendix, pages A66-A74).

Prevatt Lake

Land-based Stationary Resistivity Profiles

Prevatt Lake is located within the Wekiwa Springs State Park in Orange County. The 112-m-long cable was positioned at four different locations and nine profiles were acquired (fig. 50; appen-

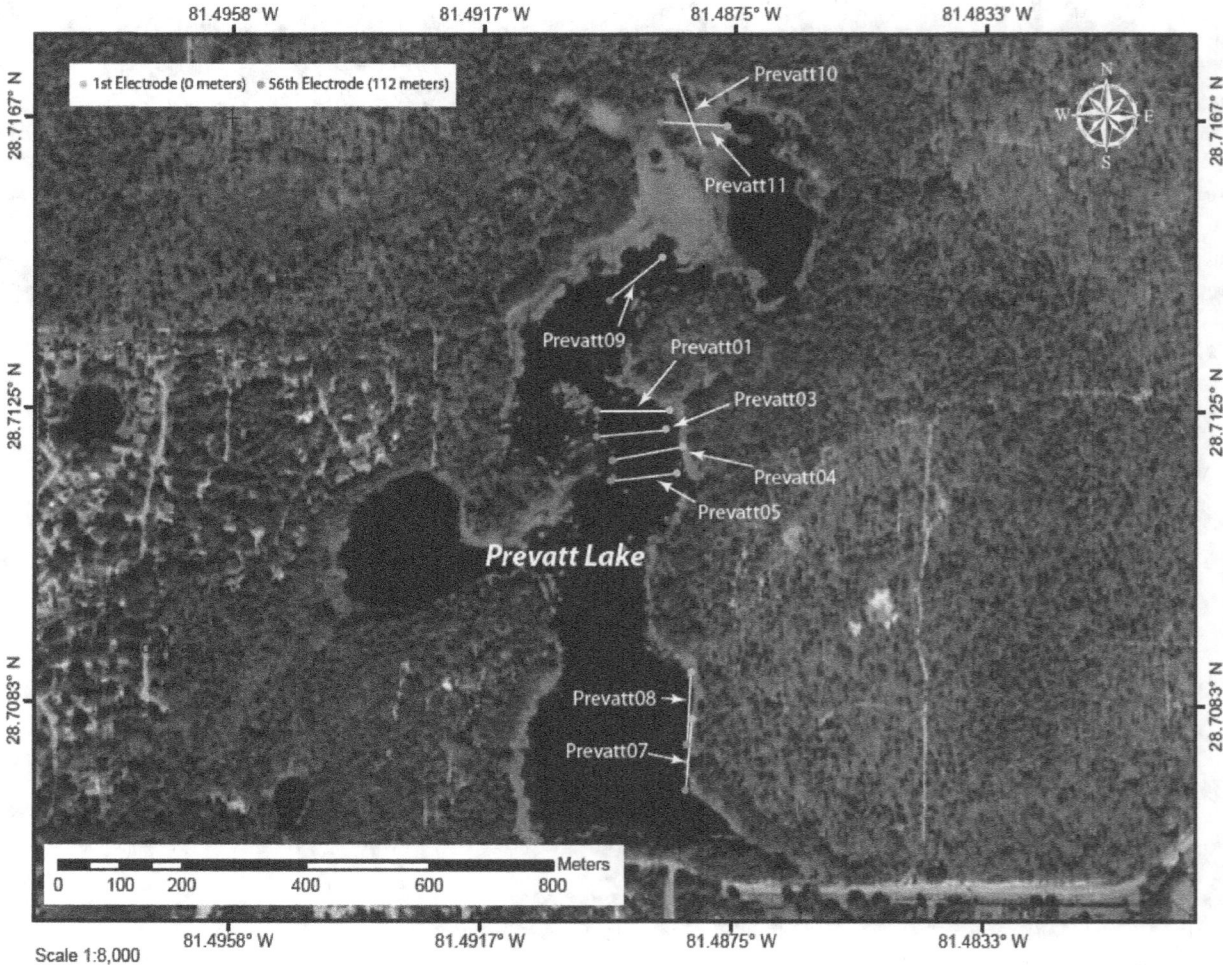

Figure 50. Location of land-based resistivity lines for Prevatt Lake. Green dot represents first electrode (0 m) and red dot represents last electrode (112 m).

dix, pages A75-A85). The four different areas were north shore (lines 10, 11), transition zone between north and middle ponds (line 9), central area (lines 1, 3, 4, 5), and southern shore (lines 7, 8).

Two intersecting lines (Prevatt 10, 11) along the northern area of Prevatt Lake show a relatively thick (<12 m) resistive unit (~480 ohm-m), most likely composed of quartz sand, superimposed on less resistive materials (~72-180 ohm-m) that could represent silty sands or clays (appendix, pages A84-A85). The western end of line 11 shows a thinning of the resistive unit and a thickening of a conductive unit. The end of line 11 was near a small pond-like water feature. Thus, the conductive unit could represent the rim of a sinkhole.

The resistivity profile in line 9, located in the transition zone from the northern pond to the central pond, shows a typical sediment-filled sinkhole (appendix, page A83). The profile shows that a thin resistive unit (sand) is superimposed on a thick sequence of conductive materials (~36 ohm-m) from 0 to 72 m. The end of the profile (72-112 m) identifies a sinkhole feature by the abrupt downward dip in the conductive sediments and a thickening of the overlying sediments.

The central portion of Prevatt Lake shows high-resistivity material (quartz sand) overlying less resistive silty sands and clays similar to that shown in the Prevatt_09 profile (appendix, pages A76-A79). However, it is interesting to note that when the conductive bodies are identified on the profiles, they trend in a linear northwest-southeast direction and thus may represent a rim or linear structural feature. Inasmuch as the conductive units align in a trending direction, so do the sagging resistive units. The resistive units appear as bowl-shaped features that align in the same northwest-southeast direction and may represent an infilled fault/fracture zone or remnants of solution sinkholes.

Resistivity profiles were also collected along the southern shore of Prevatt Lake near previously drilled SJRWMD well sites (OR0895 AND OR0896) that have records of lithologic descriptions and geophysical logs. Prevatt 07 and 08 lines were collected individually and then merged to produce one continuous electrical resistivity profile (fig. 51; appendix, pages A80-A82). As mentioned, the ideal situation for conducting DC resistivity surveys is to have prior information to confirm the resistivity profiles. The results from borehole gamma logs and lithologic descriptions from wells OR0896 and OR0893 and the resistivity profile, taken lakeward of the wells, show a very good correlation. The resistivity profile shows a thin, high-resistivity unit (moderately dry quartz sand) overlying a conductive unit that varies in depth and thickness. The gamma-log plots have been placed on the resistivity profile to show that multiple geophysical tools can be used to identify or verify lithologic units (fig. 51). The gamma-log record from well OR0893 shows a peak at ~8 m below land surface and is positioned on top of the conductive clay unit seen in the resistivity profile. The gamma log from well OR0896 shows a deeper conductive unit with a peak in gamma at ~17 m. For illustration purposes, the gamma-log profile from well OR0896 is plotted near the 0-m mark on the resistivity profile, but in actuality it is located approximately 30 m to the north (fig. 51). At a depth of 12 m, the resistivity profile shows a thicker and deeper conductive unit from about the

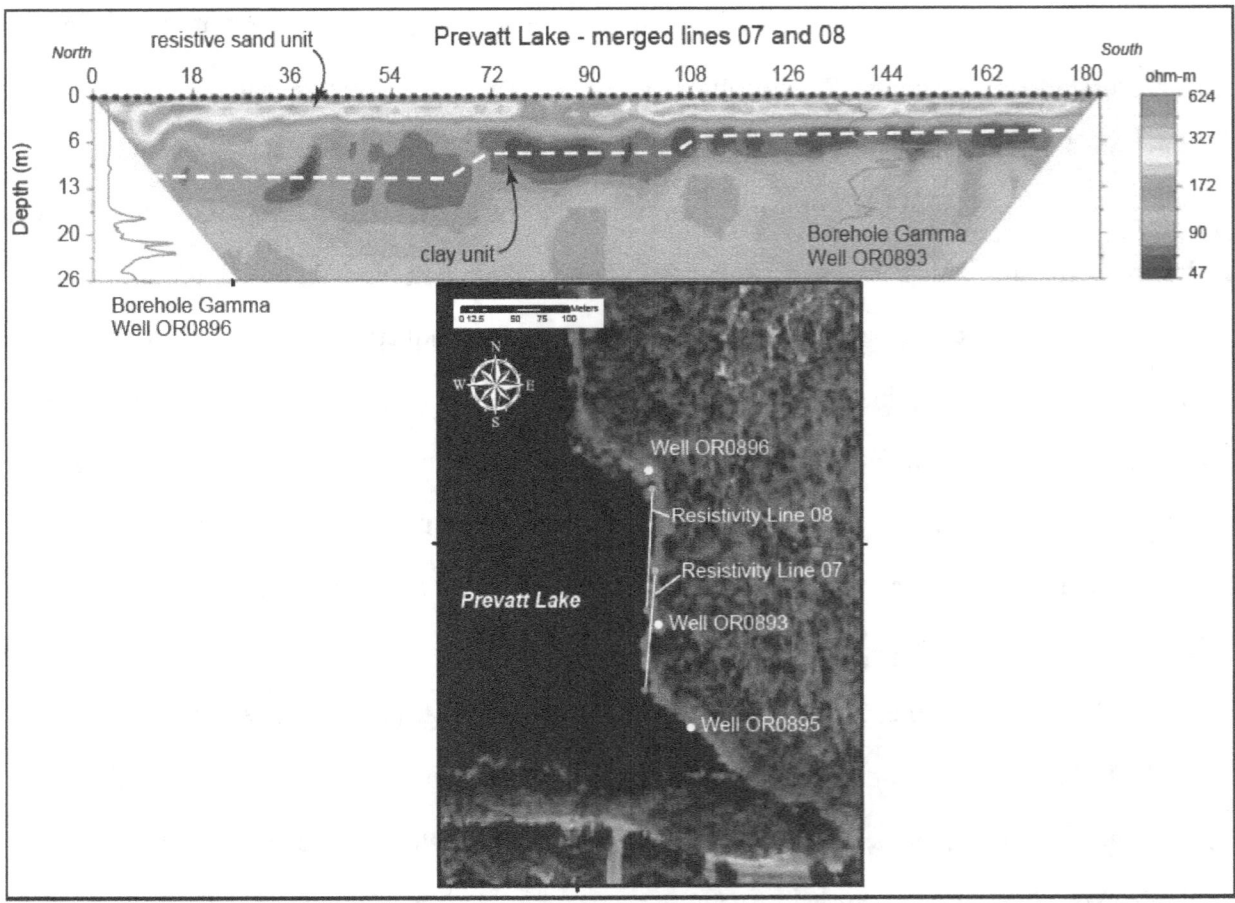

Figure 51. Resistivity profile of merged lines 07 and 08 and SJRWMD borehole gamma logs along southeast corner of Prevatt Lake. Profile shows a shallowing of the conductive clay unit (dark blue) from north to south with the dashed white line indicating the approximate center of the conductive unit. Ohm-m, ohm meters.

72-m position northward. In addition, Ocala Limestone pinnacles may be represented as mid-resistive units in the middle section of the profile (~170 ohm-m) because limestone was encountered at a depth of ~18 m by the SJRWMD during drilling of well OR0893. Limestone was not encountered within this depth during drilling of well OR0896.

Lake Saunders

Seismic Profiles

Lake Saunders is located in Lake County between Lakes Dora and Eustis. Lake Saunders is composed of a larger depression offset from a sinkhole lake on the western flank. Seismic-

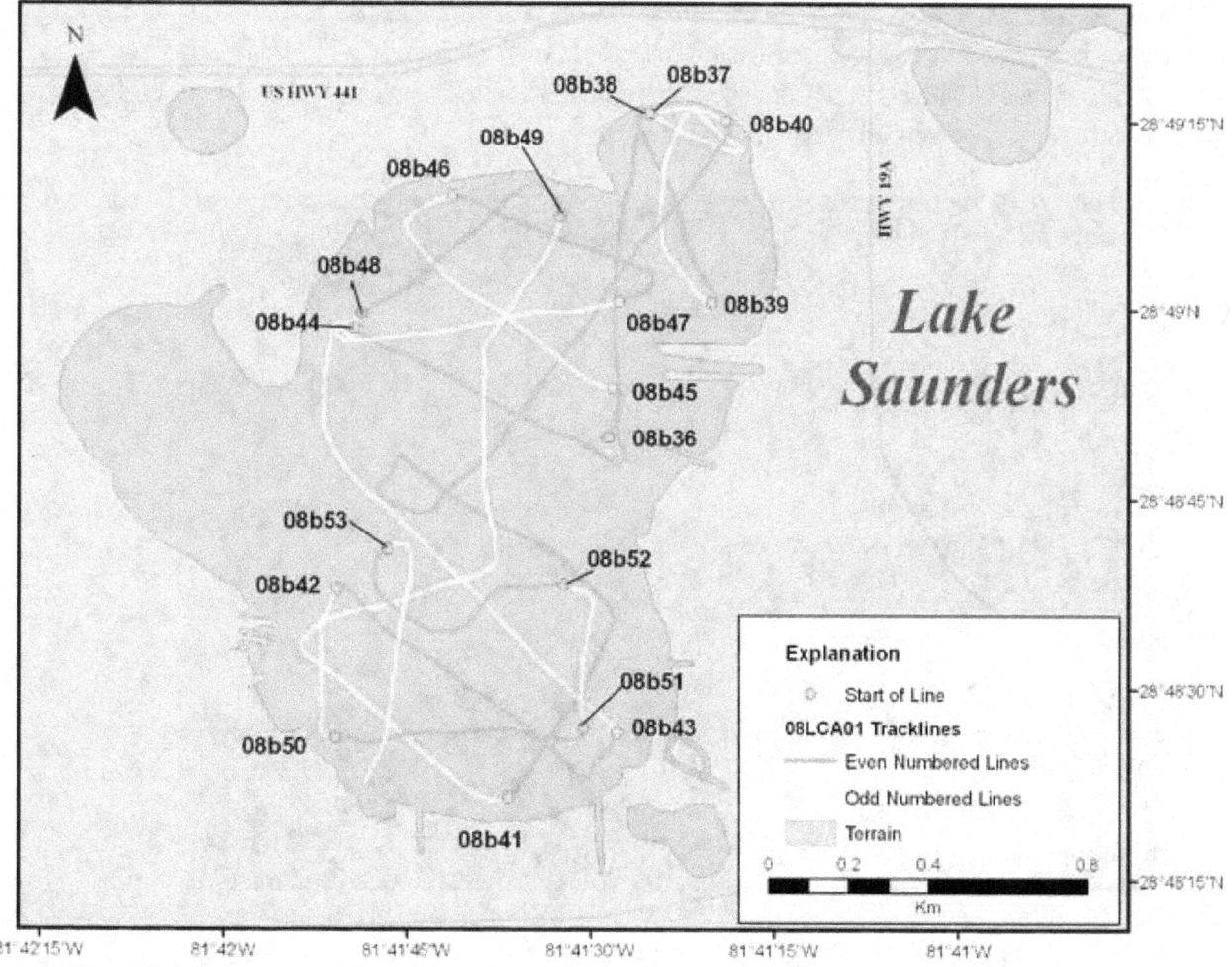

Figure 52. Seismic-profile tracklines in Lake Saunders.

47

profile tracklines in Lake Saunders are shown in figure 52. The profiles (for example, 08b43 and 08b49) show that the lake comprises several surface depressions that are related to deformation in

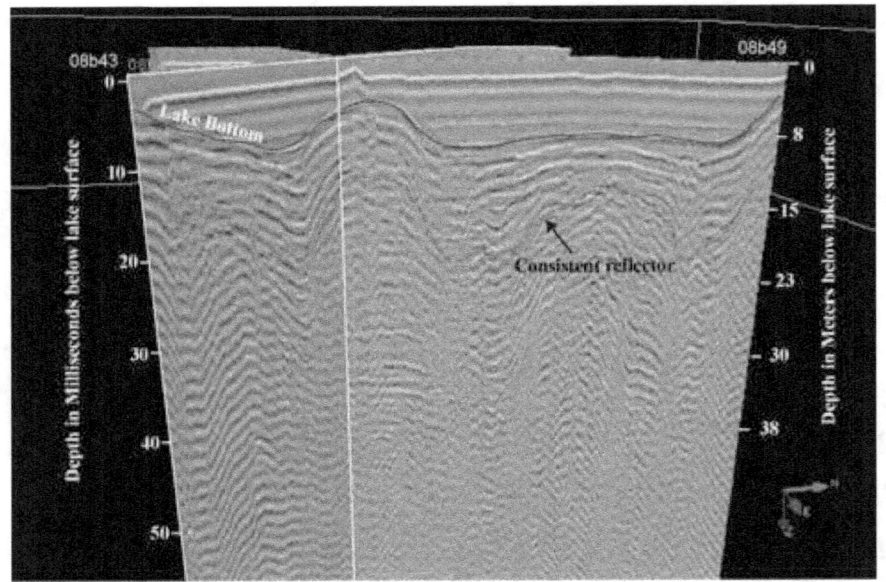

Figure 53. Seismic profile (08b43 and 08b49) collected in Lake Saunders. Locations of lines 08b43 and 08b49 are shown in figure 52. Depressions at the lake bottom are influenced by deformation at depth.

the substrate (fig. 53).

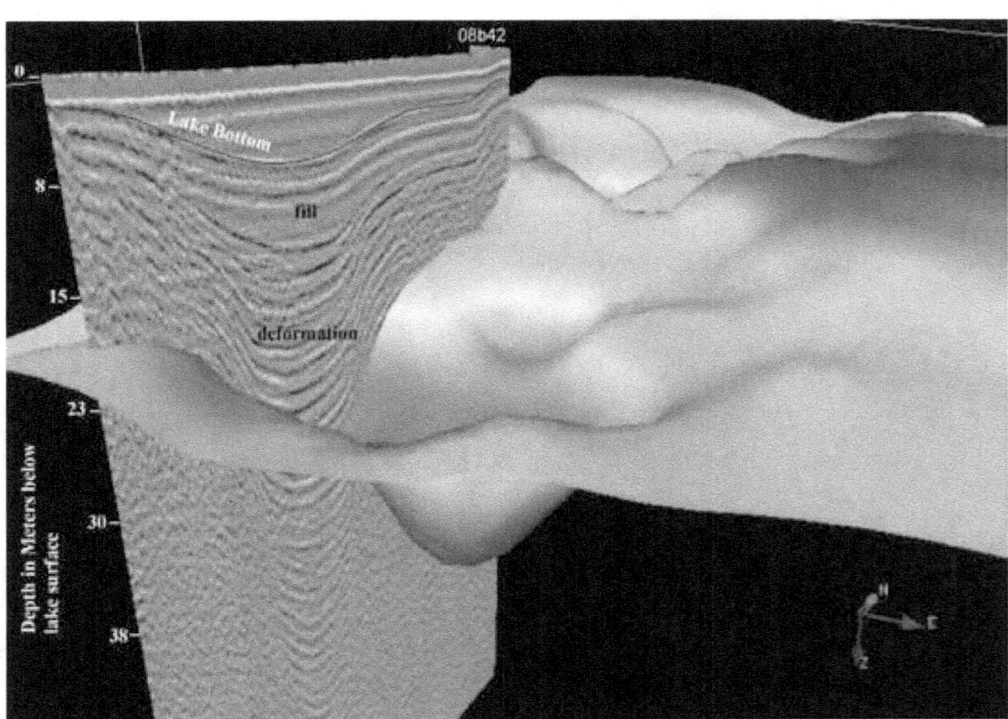

Figure 54. Three-dimensional perspective of a structural horizon below Lake Saunders, interpreted from seismic profiles, characteristic of a karst surface. Vertical scale shows depth below lake surface in meters.

Pronounced

48

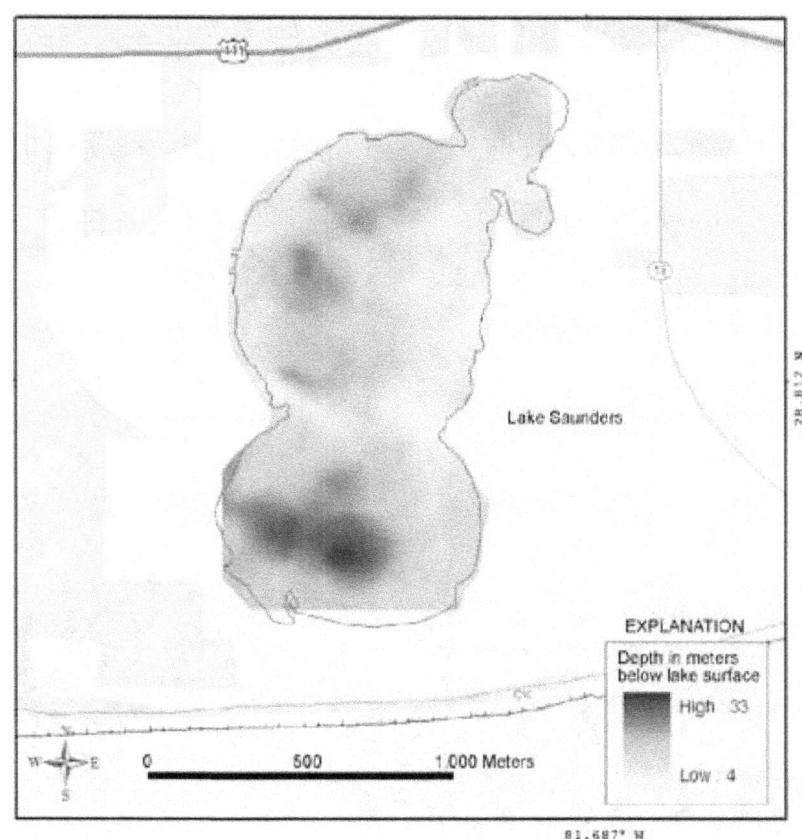

Figure 55. Color-shaded relief map of a structural horizon below Lake Saunders, interpreted from seismic profiles. (See red line in figure 53.)

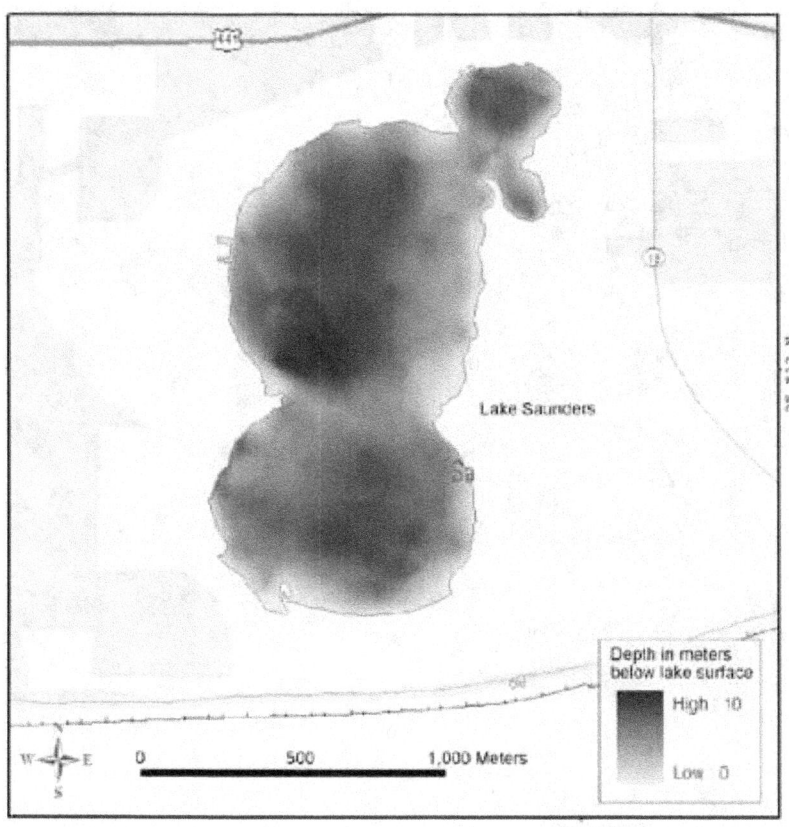

Figure 56. Bathymetric map of Lake Saunders, interpreted from seismic profiles. Refer to figure 52 for trackline coverage because not all of the lake was surveyed.

down-dipping reflectors provide a consistent pattern across the lake (fig. 54). This horizon may be associated with collapse within the Ocala Limestone and the infilling of the Hawthorn Group sediments into the depression. A color-shaded relief map of this horizon (fig. 55) shows several locations across the western side of the lake with high relief in the subsurface reflector. The lake bottom is slightly influenced by the subsurface relief and shows similar depressions (fig. 56).

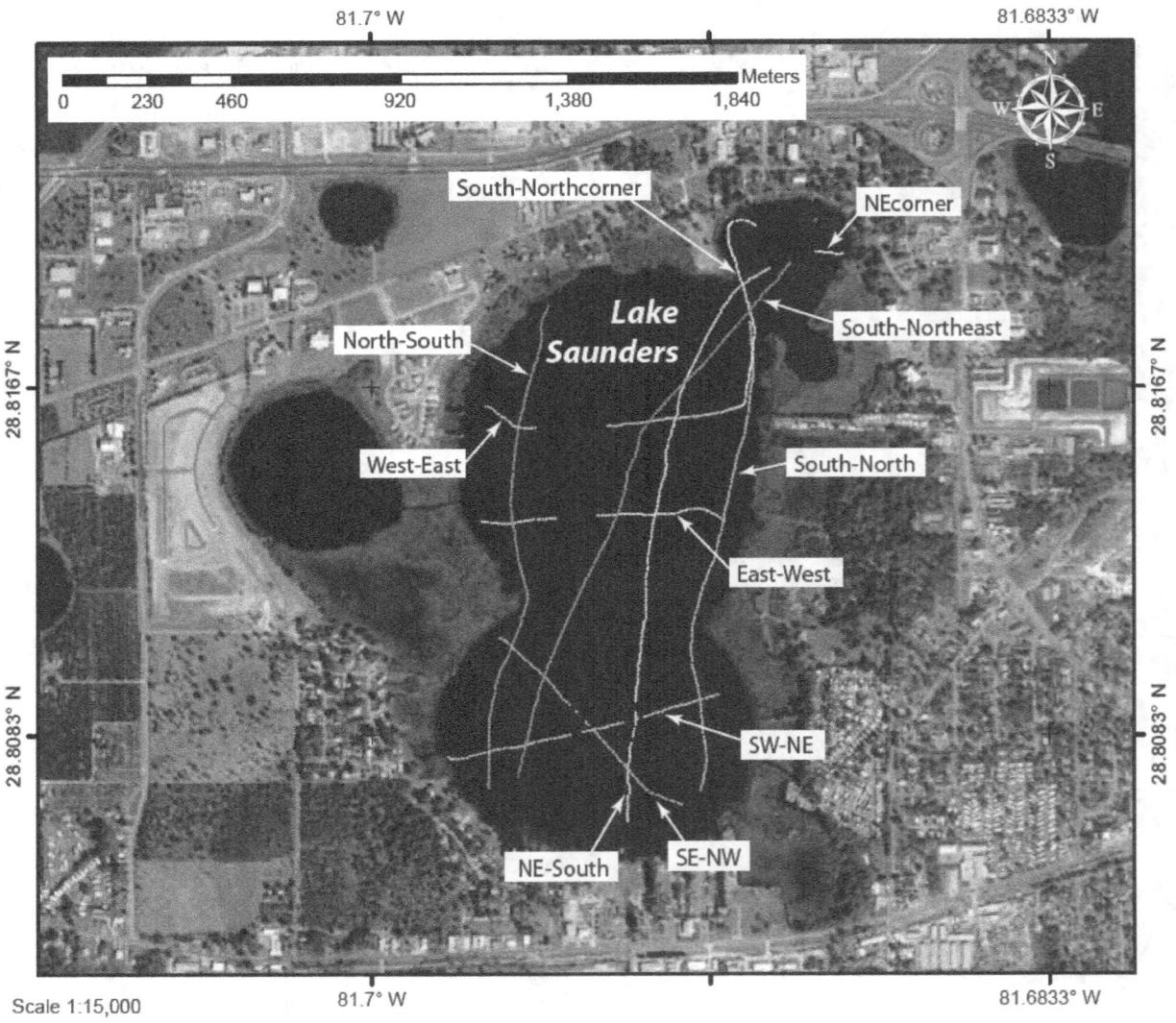

Figure 57. Continuous resistivity profile tracklines for Lake Saunders.

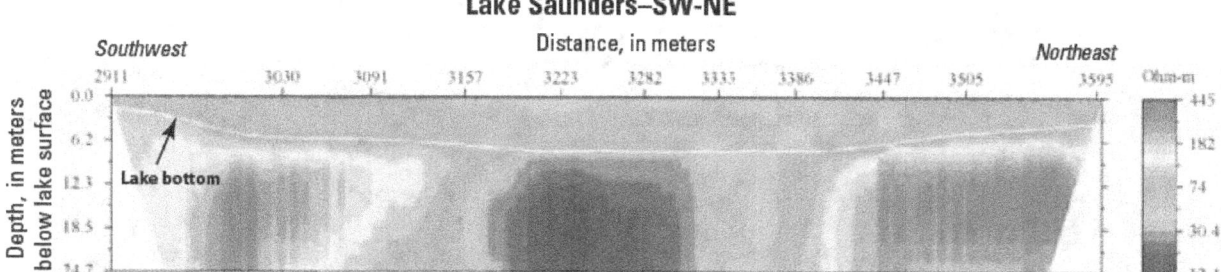

Figure 58. Resistivity profile of Saunders_SW-NE in the southern portion of Lake Saunders shows low-resistivity material infilling a sinkhole feature. Ohm-m, ohm meters.

Continuous Resistivity Profiles

Imagery from aerial photography (fig. 57) indicates that the main section of Lake Saunders was formed from the collapse of two large and one small sinkholes. Resistivity data support this concept in that two larger areas of the main lake appear to be ravel zones or areas of decreased resistivity (appendix, pages A86-A96). The southern area of the lake has a well-defined zone where resistivity shifts abruptly from ~400 ohm-m along the edges to ~12 ohm-m in the center (line Lake Saunders_SE-NW; fig. 58). The low-resistivity section may indicate an increase in porosity or clay content. A similar observation is made in the northern portion of the lake along the west-east and east-west transects. The northeast section also appears to have a similar resistivity profile with high resistivity along the rim and low resistivity in the center.

Sylvan Lake

Continuous Resistivity Profiles

Sylvan Lake is located in the northwest section of Seminole County. Sylvan Lake Recreational Park is located along the western part of the lake, and numerous residential lots occupy the southern and northeastern shore (fig. 59). Approximately 7.5 line-km of resistivity data were collected in Sylvan Lake. Resistivity data show that the subsurface of the lake consists of relatively high-resistivity material (~250 ohm-m) with isolated low-resistivity zones (appendix, pages A97-A105). The low-resistivity zones do not appear to have any structural shape and are therefore difficult to

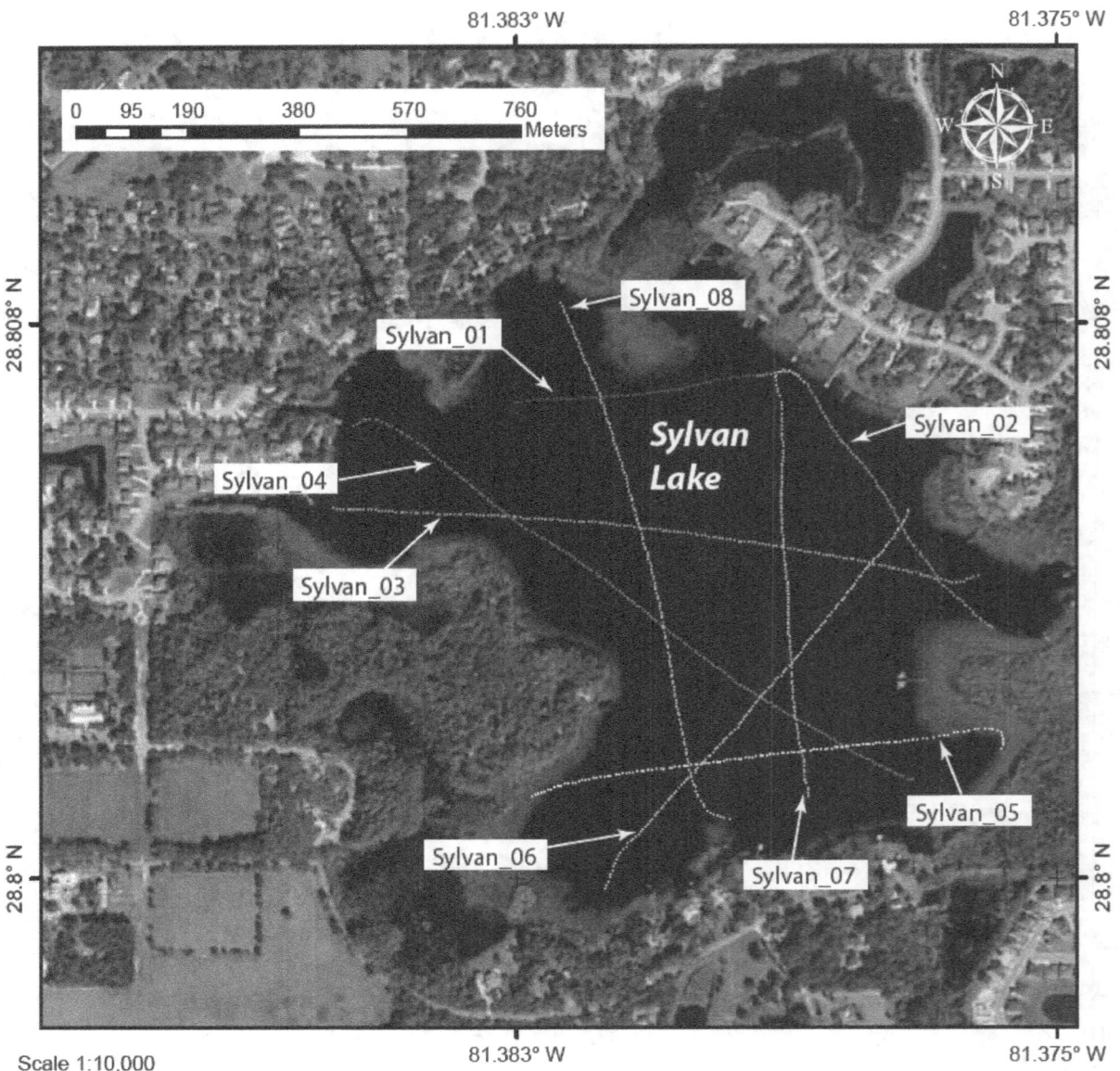

Figure 59. Continuous resistivity profile tracklines for Sylvan Lake.

interpret as karst features. Broad areas of highly resistive materials indicate that the lake is underlain predominantly with sand, though areas of clay and silty sands may be present.

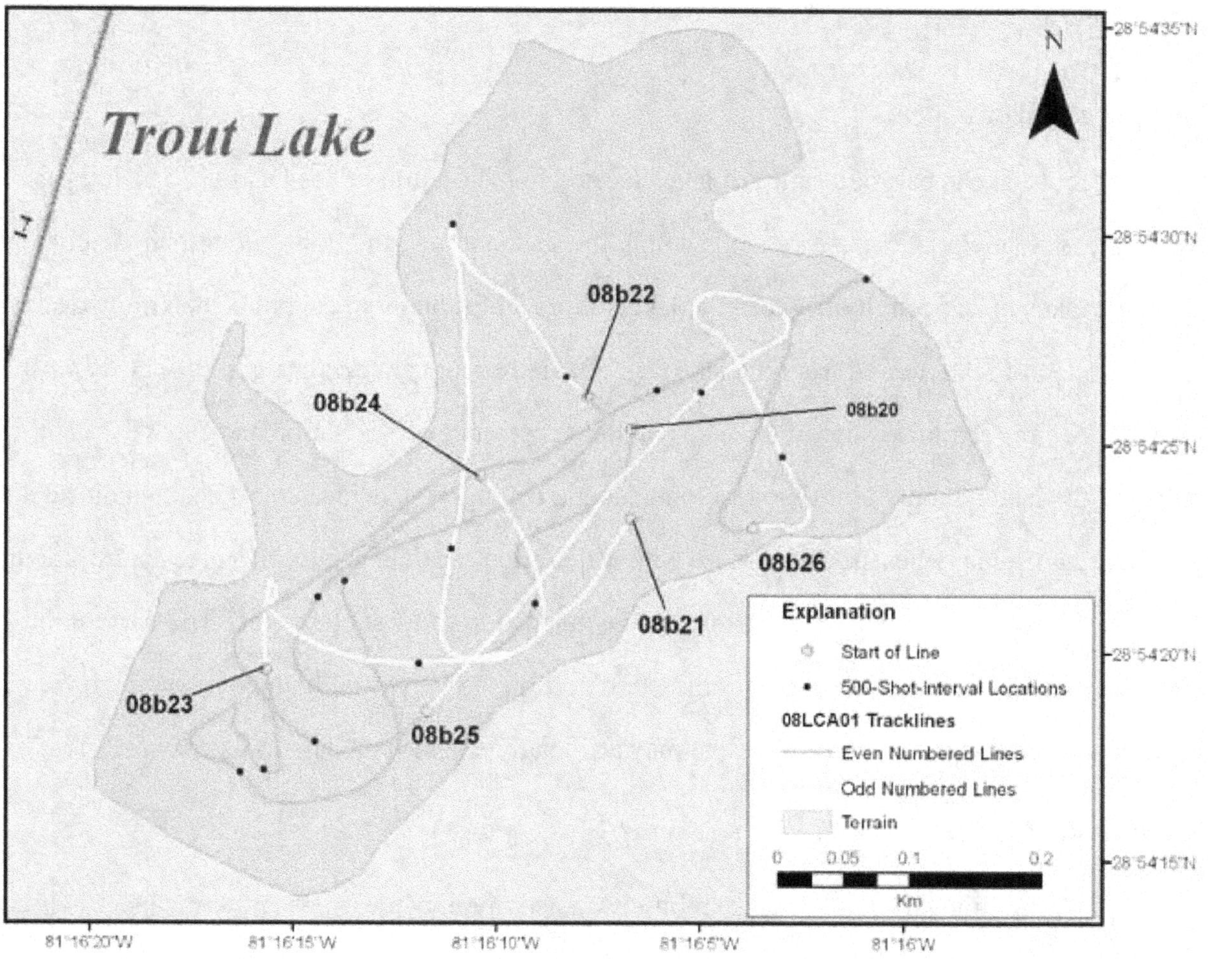

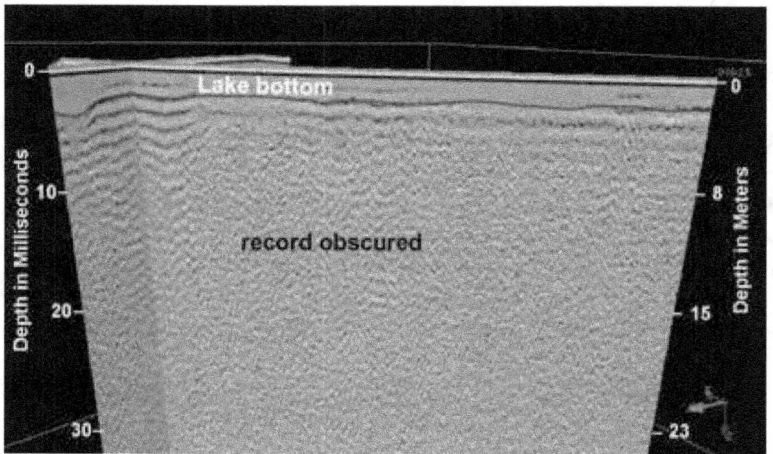

Figure 60. Seismic-profile tracklines in Trout Lake.

Figure 61. Seismic profile (08b25) collected in Trout Lake. Location of line 08b25 is shown in figure 60. Seismic record is obscured throughout the data, most likely a result of shallow water and vegetation attenuating the acoustic signal.

Trout Lake

Seismic Profiles

Trout Lake is part of a series of lakes located in the Central Lakes District. The irregular shoreline is characteristic of depressions within the surrounding sand hills, rather than the circular sinkhole lakes. Connectivity between the lake bottom and subbottom cannot be determined because the seismic profiles acquired from the lake (fig. 60) are obscured at depth (fig. 61). This is most likely due to the shallow water of the lake and to the presence of vegetation and detrital organic material on the lake bottom. Housing development and the highway adjacent to the lake indicate that much of the lake may be associated more with water retention than a natural depression. Although difficult to resolve, lake-bottom reflectors can be mapped to show subtle relief. The data might indicate a shallow depression in the northeastern portion of the lake, although with a low level of confidence because a turn in the trackline may artificially enhance the lake-bottom expression.

Lake Hydrology

Determining why some lakes exhibit low resistivity in depressions and some lakes exhibit high resistivity in similar structures will aid in the understanding of why certain lake water levels vary more or less than levels of other lakes in a similar physiographic area. The ultimate goal of this study was to provide additional performance measures, specifically geologic information, on establishment of minimum flows and levels (MFLs) criteria for individual lakes and water bodies. This study has shown that each lake surveyed exhibits its own geologic complexity. Geologic data in proximity to each lake (for example, gamma-log profiles and geologist logs) will provide relative thickness of overburden, an important factor when comparing subsidence- to collapse-type sinkholes. The next step is to determine whether or not lake water-level fluctuations can be linked to subsidence- or collapse-type sinkhole formations. Based on the limited number of lakes surveyed, it appears that there may be a link between lake formation and fluctuations in lake water levels. For example, the water level in Lake Saunders, identified as a possible collapse-sinkhole lake, does not fluctuate as greatly as water levels in Lake Avalon, Johns Lake, Lake Helen, or Lake Colby, which

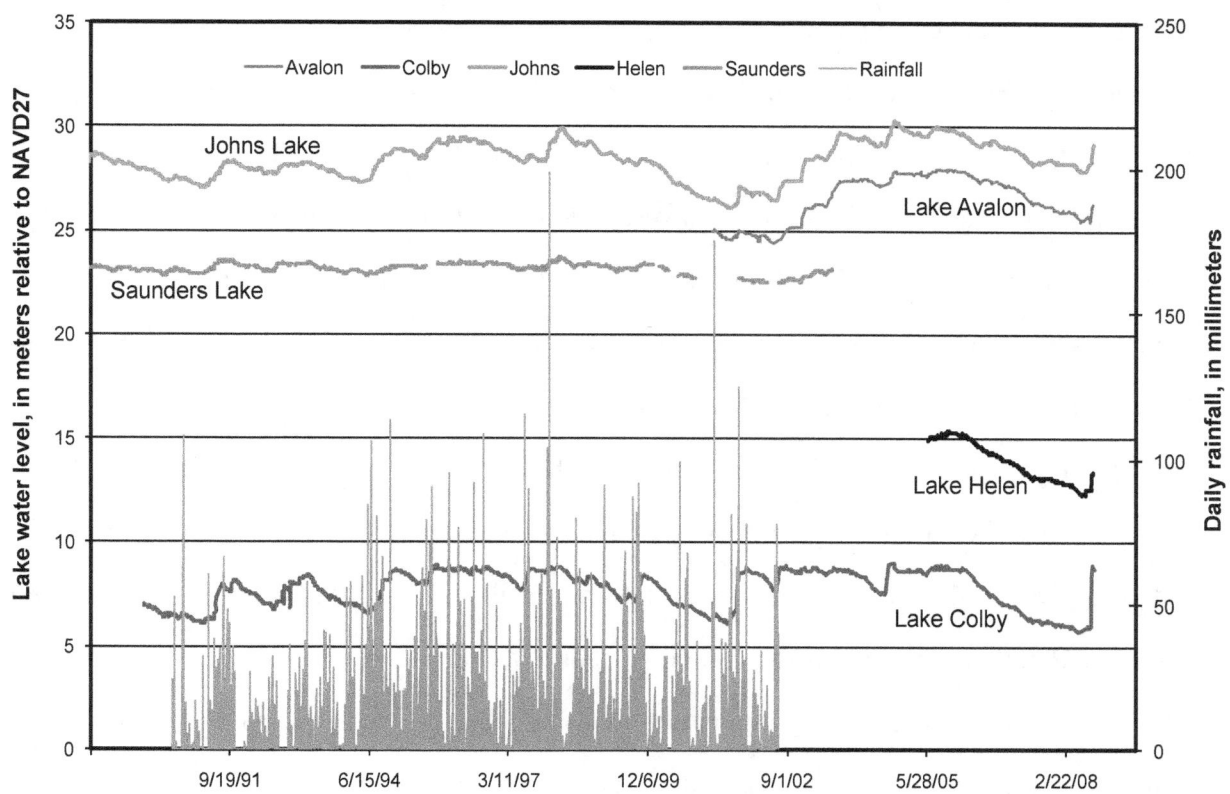

Figure 62. Surface-water elevations for select sentinel lakes surveyed in this study, and rainfall from nearby Lake Helen. (Data from the SJRWMD data-portal Web site.)

have been identified as possible subsidence-sinkhole lakes (fig. 62). Lake Saunders water level has only fluctuated ~3 ft over the 17 years of data collected. Avalon, Johns, Helen, and Colby water records show a much greater fluctuation, with averages of 11 ft, 13 ft, 10 ft, and 11 ft, respectively. Lake Saunders is physically separated from Helen, Colby, Johns, and Avalon. To test this hypothesis further, a few additional lakes near Saunders need to be investigated.

Summary

High-resolution seismic-profiling data collected from numerous lakes in central Florida show comparable acoustic patterns among lakes. Most of the lakes in the study exhibit one or more depressions on the lake bottom that are associated with similar deformation in the subbottom. The patterns indicate collapse at depth within the Ocala Limestone, and deformation of the overlying Hawthorn Group sediments into the collapse feature. In some of the lakes, parallel reflectors in the near surface indicate fill material in the depression. This relation among collapse, deformation, and fill is supported by continuous resistivity profiles acquired in the lakes that show differential resistance within the lake material. The use of high-resolution seismic and direct-current resistivity in this study has provided insight that a single geophysical tool alone could not have provided. It is known that the lakes studied during this investigation were formed by sinkholes, but this study has shown that there are two variations on lake composition and structure. The first is a lake in which high-resistivity materials occur in troughs or depressions (for example, Avalon, Johns, Helen and Colby Lakes). These high-resistivity materials are most likely clean quartz sands that have been carried into depressions from deep limestone-karst formation. The second type of lake has low-resistivity material infilling a depression or trough. The occurrence of this type of lake exemplifies sediment ravel, or the process of materials and water infilling a collapse structure. The end result is an increase in matrix porosity that therefore leads to a decrease in resistivity (for example, Lake Saunders). Though based on a low statistical number of samples (n=5), it appears that there is a link in the type of lake formation and water-level fluctuations. Further processing and interpretation of existing data will provide additional correlation between acoustic and electrical resistivity response in karst environments and will provide a strategy for continued analysis in the region, in conjunction with land-based borings and geophysical measurements.

Acknowledgments

The St. Johns River Water Management District (SJRWMD) provided funding for this study. Personnel from the U.S. Geological Survey St. Petersburg Coastal and Marine Science Center provided field support, data processing, and assisted in creating the report. The authors thank Dana Wiese and Jordan Sanford for field support, Shawn Dadisman and Arnell Harrison for data processing and archive development, and Kathryn Smith for GIS support. Peter Swarzenski provided resistivity equipment. Appreciation is extended to Noreen Buster, Rick Spechler, and Barbara Lidz for critical reviews of this report.

References Cited

Barry, K.M., Cavers, D.A., and Kneale, C.W., 1975, Recommended standards for digital tape formats: Geophysics, v. 40, no. 2, p. 344-352.

Beck, B.F., 1988, Environmental and engineering effects of sinkholes: The processes behind the problems: Environmental Geology and Water Science, v. 12, no 2, p. 71-78.

Day-Lewis, F.D., White, E.A., Belaval, M., Johnson, C.D., and Lane, J.W., 2006, Continuous resistivity profiling to delineate submarine ground-water discharge—examples and limitations: The Leading Edge, v. 25, no. 6, p. 724-728.

Dobecki, T.L., and Upchurch, S.B., 2006, Geophysical applications to detect sinkholes and ground subsidence: The Leading Edge, v. 25, no. 3, p. 336-341.

Flocks, J.G., Kindinger, J.L., Davis, J.B., and Swarzenski, P.W., 2001, Geophysical investigations of upward migrating saline water from the lower to upper Floridan Aquifer, central Indian River region, Florida, *in* Kunianksy, E.L., ed., U.S. Geological Survey Karst Interest Group Proceedings, St. Petersburg, Florida, February 13-16, 2001: U.S. Geological Survey Water-Resources Investigations Report 01-4011, p. 135-140.

Harrison, A.S., Dadisman, S.V., Flocks, J.G., Wiese, D.S., and Robbins, L.L., 2007, Archive of digital CHIRP seismic reflection data collected during USGS cruise 06FSH01 offshore of Siesta Key, Florida, May 2006: U.S. Geological Survey Data Series, 254, DVD-ROM.

Harrison, A.S., Dadisman, S.V., Davis, J.B., Flocks, J.G. and Wiese, D.S., 2009a, Archive of digital boomer seismic reflection data collected during USGS field activity 08LCA01 in 10 central Florida lakes, March 2008: U.S. Geological Survey Data Series 421, DVD-ROM.

Harrison, A.S., Dadisman, S.V., Davis, J.B., Flocks, J.G. and Wiese, D.S., 2009b, Archive of Digital Boomer Seismic Reflection Data Collected During USGS Field Activity 08LCA04 in Lakes Cherry, Helen, Hiawassee, Louisa, and Prevatt, Central Florida, September 2008 USGS Data Series: 445, DVD-ROM

Kindinger, J.L., 2002, Lake belt study area: High-resolution seismic reflection survey, Miami-Dade County Florida: U.S. Geological Survey Open-File Report 02-325, CD-ROM.

Kindinger, J.L., Davis, J.B., and Flocks, J.G., 1994, High-resolution single-channel seismic reflection surveys of Orange Lake and other selected sites of north central Florida: U.S. Geological Survey Open-File Report 94-616, CD-ROM.

Kindinger, J.L., Davis, J.B., and Flocks, J.G., 1999, Geology and evolution of lakes in north-central Florida: Environmental Geology, v. 38, no. 4, p. 301-321.

Kindinger, J.L., Davis, J.B., and Flocks, J.G., 2000, Subsurface characterization of selected water bodies in the St. Johns River Water Management District, Northeast Florida: U.S. Geological Survey Open-File Report 00-180, CD-ROM.

Reich, C.D., Swarzenski, P.W., Kindinger, J.L., Flocks, J.G., Hickey, T.D., and Spechler, R.M., 2001, Direct linkages between onshore karst aquifers and offshore marine environments, Crescent Beach Spring, Florida, *in* Kunianksy, E.L., ed., U.S. Geological Survey Karst Interest Group Proceedings, St. Petersburg, Florida, February 13-16, 2001: U.S. Geological Survey Water-Resources Investigations Report 01-4011, p. 106.

Sacks, L.A., Lee, T.M., and Tihansky, A.B., 1991, Hydrogeologic setting and preliminary data analysis for the hydrologic-budget assessment of Lake Barco, an acidic seepage lake in Putnam County, Florida: U.S. Geological Survey Water-Resources Investigations Report 91-4180, 28 p.

Schiffer, D.M., 1998, Hydrology of central Florida lakes—A primer: U.S. Geological Survey Circular 1137, 38 p.

St. Johns River Water Management District (SJRWMD), 2008, Minimum flows and levels: Priority list and schedule: St. Johns River Water Management District 2008 Consolidated Annual Report, 9 p.

Wiener, J.M., 1982, Geologic modeling in the Lake Wauberg-Chacala Pond vicinity utilizing seismic refraction techniques: University of Florida, Gainesville, Florida, M.S. thesis, 94 p.